Navigating the First Year
of Law School

Navigating the First Year of Law School

A Practical Guide to Studying Law

G. Nicholas Herman
Melissa A. Essary
Zachary C. Bolitho

Contributor
Brady N. Herman

CAROLINA ACADEMIC PRESS
Durham, North Carolina

Library of Congress Cataloging-in-Publication Data

Names: Herman, G. Nicholas, author. | Essary, Melissa A., author. |
Bolitho, Zachary C., author.
Title: Navigating the first year of law school : a practical guide to
studying law / G. Nicholas Herman, Melissa A. Essary, and
Zachary C. Bolitho.
Description: Durham, North Carolina : Carolina Academic Press,
2016. |
Includes bibliographical references and index.
Identifiers: LCCN 2016019812 (print) | LCCN 2016020780 (ebook) |
ISBN 9781611639575 (alk. paper) | ISBN 9781531001346 (ebook)
Subjects: LCSH: Law--Study and teaching--United States. | Law
students--United States--Handbooks, manuals, etc.
Classification: LCC KF283 .H47 2016 (print) | LCC KF283 (ebook) |
DDC 340.071/173--dc23
LC record available at https://lccn.loc.gov/2016019812

Carolina Academic Press, LLC
700 Kent Street
Durham, NC 27701
Telephone (919) 489-7486
Fax (919) 493-5668
www.cap-press.com

This book is dedicated to:

My law students who taught me what to say in this book.
—GNH

My parents, Delwin and Barbara Webb, who taught me by example.
—MAE

My grandparents, Don and Helen Wright, for all of their
love and encouragement.
—ZCB

Contents

Preface

If you are an entering law student, this book is for you. It provides you with what you will need to know in order to be successful in law school. More specifically, it covers:

- How lawyers use the law
- How the legal system works
- The basics of how to study
- How to read case decisions
- How to write case briefs
- How to participate in class
- How to prepare detailed course outlines
- How to use common sense when thinking about the law
- How to study for exams and write essay exam answers
- How to make the most of your first year

In addition, the book contains a chapter with some pointers about how to research and write a memorandum of law. This chapter will be useful to you only *after* you have first learned the basic mechanics of legal research. The subject is included because of the difficulty and importance of research and writing in the first-year curriculum.

This book is also designed to be read in advance of, or in connection with, a law school orientation program that introduces you to the study of law. It covers the conventional topics and instruction given by law professors about studying law. In this way, the book is intended to complement and enhance the tutelage that you are given in an orientation program about how to approach your studies and what to expect during your first year.

—GNH; MAE; ZCB

Acknowledgments

The authors gratefully acknowledge the following individuals for their review and contributions to this book: Andrew Ackley, Esq.; Professor Nim Batchelor; Matthew Bissette; Olivia Bouffard; Professor Lance Burke; Professor Patti Bynum; Tripp Choate; Brennan Cumalander; Professor Shelly DeAdder; Professor Catherine Dunham; Sarah Fishel; Spencer Fritts; Professor Brenda Gibson; Reggie Gillespie, Esq.; Kevin Hornik; Nancy Hornik, Esq.; Karl Lockhart; Allison Long; T.C. Morphis, Esq.; Professor Mark Morris; Claudia Mundy; Hathaway Pendergrass, Esq.; Cody Porter; Dr. Tom Porter, Ph.D.

Navigating the First Year
of Law School

Chapter 1

How to Read This Book

> *If you are resolutely determined to make a lawyer of your-self, the thing is more than half done already.*
> —*Abraham Lincoln*

We have designed this book to help you understand what the first year of law school is all about. You should read this book before you start law school, preferably in June or July. If you read this book and take its advice to heart, we believe you will be better prepared to confront the rigors of law school.

In this book, you will first learn how lawyers use the law. And you will gain an overview of the legal system. This will set the stage for what you will study in your first year. The book then turns to the basics of how to study, how to read and brief case decisions, how to participate in class, how to prepare course outlines, and how to use common sense in your studies. It will also provide some pointers on how to research and write a memorandum of law, how to study for exams, how to write effective exam answers, and how to make the most of your first year. As the title makes clear, this book is a guide that will help you navigate the difficult terrain of law school.

You will benefit most from this book if you read the chapters in order. We suggest that you avoid the temptation to selectively skip from one chapter to another. There is one exception to this suggestion: hold off reading Chapter 10 on "How to Research & Write a Memorandum of Law" until *after* you have first learned the basic mechanics of legal research in your *Legal Re-*

search and Writing course and have been assigned to research and write your first Memorandum of Law.

After you have read the book, you might find it useful to re-read certain chapters from time to time during law school. For example, if you are frustrated by the use of the Socratic Method in class, you can re-read the chapter about "How to Participate in Class." Similarly, the chapter on "How to Study for Exams & Write Law School Exam Answers" will be useful to re-read before you take your first exam. While this book is short, it's packed with helpful advice. Take advantage of it.

There is a lot of lore about the first year of law school. You may hear from various corners that your first year is "extremely hard," "unbearably time-consuming," and "hugely stressful." Those characterizations are undoubtedly true for some people and overstated for others. What is universal, however, is the fact that the first year of law school is different from any academic endeavor you have previously experienced. That is why we have written this book—to help prepare you for law school. And, knowing what to expect when you walk into your first law school class will reduce your stress level.

Many first-year students find themselves misguided by incomplete or erroneous advice provided by second- or third-year students, lawyer friends, or others who purport to have heard or read about law school. While all of those people may be well-meaning and some of their advice may be excellent, in this book you will hear it directly from "the horse's mouth"— law professors. If your law school provides you with an orientation program, you should certainly soak up and apply the advice provided there, along with everything described in this book. Don't hesitate to engage with this book. Interact with it. Put your pen or pencil to the paper: underline or highlight important points, circle new words, make notes in the margins. Have at it.

If you carefully follow the advice in this book, you will be prepared to effectively study law from the first day of classes, and you won't waste time figuring out how to study. This does not mean that your first year will be easy. The law and the analytical skills associated with understanding and applying the law will be new to you and, therefore, very challenging at the outset. If you fully understand how to approach your studies from the first day of classes and if you work hard, we believe you will find your first year of law school to be intellectually stimulating, rewarding, and manageable. Indeed, you may find yourself saying, "It's the hardest thing I've ever done, but I love it."

Chapter 2

How Lawyers Use the Law

Synopsis

2.01 What Lawyers Do
2.02 Sources of the Law

> *A lawyer's advice is his stock in trade.*
>
> —*Abraham Lincoln*

Law school is a gateway to a broad array of careers. When you enter law school, you may be interested in a specific area of the law or type of law practice. However, students often enter law school without knowing exactly what they will do with their law degree upon graduation. This is entirely normal.

Many students, including those who begin their studies with a specific legal career in mind, find that their legal interests evolve during law school. Just as an entering medical student with an interest in becoming a surgeon might later choose to become a neurologist, an entering law student with an interest in business law might later choose to become a criminal defense lawyer. Law school helps you discover your unique talents and interests in the law, with the result that your ultimate service as a lawyer may be quite different from what you envisioned at the outset.

This chapter begins with an overview of what lawyers do. It then discusses the basic sources of law used in the legal profession.

2.01 What Lawyers Do

Lawyers generally represent clients. And clients come to lawyers for all sorts of reasons. As a lawyer, you might help a client prepare a will, purchase a home, or set up a new business. A client might ask you to draft a piece of legislation, a contract, or an employee handbook. A client might be in trouble—charged with a crime, fired from a job, or embroiled in a bitter divorce. A client might seek your help after being sued, or a client may want to file a lawsuit after being injured in a car accident. A client might want to hire you to serve as an agent in a transaction, a negotiator in a business deal, or a spokesperson before a city council or other public body. Or a client might simply want to talk with you about the potential legal ramifications of a particular situation or plan of action. In short, a client might call upon you to serve in any number of roles—as draftsman, advocate, litigator, agent, dealmaker, negotiator, mediator, spokesperson, or general advisor.

Lawyers are trained to understand the law, to research it, and to argue about it both in writing and orally. Lawyers predict how the law will apply to the particular circumstances of a client's situation when the application of the law to that situation is unclear. In their advisory role, lawyers essentially are *problem solvers* with a special expertise in how the law affects their clients' decisions. Regardless of the type of law you practice, your client will be looking to you for guidance and good counsel. This is why many attorneys' law licenses and letterheads identify them not only as "Attorneys" but also as "Counselors at Law."

Finally, lawyers serve in many roles outside the actual practice of law. For example, lawyers serve as judges, law professors, and occasionally as college professors. Many lawyers serve as CEOs, presidents, or executives of universities, businesses, and non-profit organizations. Moreover, lawyers often serve in public service roles in Congress, state legislatures, local-government councils or boards, and in other important positions in the governmental sector. Indeed, more than half of our nation's presidents have been lawyers. In all of these roles, even if they do not involve the actual practice of law, lawyers draw upon the law and their special skills as problem solvers and counselors to make important and meaningful contributions to our society. This is why lawyers are considered members of a "noble profession."

Given the important roles that lawyers play in various sectors of society, it should come as no surprise to you that training to become a lawyer is no small task. So, buckle up and get ready to learn. Hard work and diligent study are the price of admission to a great career.

2.02   Sources of the Law

You hear the word "law" all the time. But, what exactly is the "law"? The law is found in two sources: primary authorities and secondary authorities. Primary authorities constitute the *actual* "law." These authorities are written by persons or entities empowered to make and interpret the law, such as judges through court opinions, legislatures through the enactment of statutes, and administrative agencies through the creation of rules and regulations. Secondary authorities are written by law professors, lawyers, and other experts. Secondary authorities merely explain or comment on the primary authorities of the law. Some examples of secondary authorities are treatises, hornbooks, legal encyclopedias, and law review articles.

Primary authorities consist of federal *and* state:

(1) Constitutions (the U.S. Constitution and state constitutions);

(2) Statutes (legislation enacted by Congress or state legislatures, as well as ordinances enacted by local governments such as cities and counties);

(3) <u>Rules and Regulations</u> (procedures or requirements created by various governmental entities, administrative agencies, or regulatory boards or commissions); and

(4) <u>Case Law</u> (published case decisions, usually written by judges of the appellate courts to which appeals are taken from the trial courts).

Case law is a primary authority that deserves a more thorough explanation because it will be featured so prominently in your first year of law school. Case law develops through published case decisions that interpret the meaning and application of constitutions, statutes, and rules and regulations. In addition, case law at the state level also establishes a body of law referred to as the "common law." The "common law" is made by judges through their case decisions that address legal rights, duties, and remedies not expressly covered by constitutions, statutes, and rules and regulations.

In both the federal and the state legal systems, case law establishes "precedent" under the doctrine of *stare decisis. Stare decisis* is a Latin phrase that means "to stand by things decided." Under this doctrine, when a court has published an opinion that decides a case in a certain way, future cases involving substantially similar facts and legal claims should be decided the same way. In other words, the published decision establishes a precedent for how similar future cases should be decided. Although courts occasionally overrule precedent when they conclude that prior decisions were ill-reasoned or that modern conditions now call for a different approach, *stare decisis* is designed to provide consistency, continuity, and certainty in the law.

Among the primary authorities of law, a recognized hierarchy exists. Constitutions sit atop that hierarchy, and they trump statutes, as well as rules and regulations. Just below constitutions are statutes, and they trump rules and regulations. And, rules and regulations are next, meaning that they trump the common law. Here is a summary of this hierarchy:

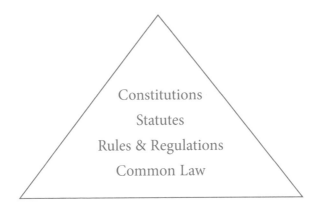

In typical first-year law school courses, you will address all of these primary sources of law. Below are some examples of the types of primary authorities you will address in your first-year courses:

- *Constitutional Law* focuses on provisions of the U.S. Constitution.
- *Civil Procedure* focuses primarily on the "Federal Rules of Civil Procedure" that govern civil lawsuits in federal court. (You may also study certain state rules of procedure that govern civil lawsuits in state courts).
- *Criminal Law, Contracts, Torts,* and *Property* focus on state common law and state statutory law.

You will regularly read case decisions on these subjects in all of your first-year courses. While your professors will teach you the substance of the law, they also will teach you how to think critically and analytically. You will often hear your professors say that they are training you "how to think like a lawyer." What does that mean? It means learning to distinguish between facts that matter and facts that don't. It means learning to take a general principle of law and explain how that general principle should apply in a new situation. It means learning to identify legal problems and developing a strategy for resolving, avoiding, or mitigating those problems. "Thinking like a lawyer" is something you will master during your law school career. It is a skill that applies the law to resolve real-life problems.

Chapter 3

How the Legal System Works

Synopsis

Laws are a dead letter without courts to expound and define their meaning and operation.

— Alexander Hamilton

Before law school starts, you will get a list of required books for your first semester. These books generally will be filled with cases decided by appellate courts throughout the country. Where did these cases come from? How did they arise? How do they fit into the law? The answers to these questions require an understanding of our legal system, which is the stage on which the law is made and practiced.

This chapter introduces you to the different types of cases in our legal system, the different courts (federal and state) that resolve those cases, and the process by which our courts decide cases from trial through appeal. *Be forewarned*: there is a lot of information and new terminology in this chapter. But stick with it. Don't become discouraged. Study the material below to get a basic understanding of the structure and process of our legal system. This will make it much easier for you to understand the other chapters in this book and, importantly, the case decisions and law you will study in your first-year courses.

3.01 The Distinction Between Civil and Criminal Cases

Our legal system provides for the judicial resolution of two kinds of legal disputes or "cases": civil and criminal. As explained below, there are important differences between civil and criminal cases. You must grasp these differences to understand how the legal system functions.

[1] Civil Cases

In a civil case, the complaining party is known as a "plaintiff." A civil case is started when the plaintiff brings a lawsuit claiming to have suffered an injury due to the fault of another person or entity. That person or entity is known as a "defendant." In the lawsuit, the plaintiff will ask the court for redress or "relief" against the defendant. For example, among other things, this relief might consist of:

- money "damages,"
- an "injunction" ordering the defendant to perform some act or to refrain from performing some act, or
- an order for a "declaratory judgment" that determines the rights or responsibilities of the parties under a legal instru-

ment (e.g., a contract, deed, or patent), or under the requirements of a constitution, statute, rule or regulation. Plaintiffs and defendants in civil cases may be individual persons, corporations, organizations, or governmental entities.

Civil lawsuits begin when a plaintiff files a "Complaint" (or "Petition") with a court that has jurisdiction over the matter and the parties involved. A complaint asserts legal "claims" (also referred to as "causes of action") based on allegations that the defendant has failed to fulfill some legal duty owed to the plaintiff or violated some legal right of the plaintiff.

For instance, the plaintiff may allege that the defendant breached a contract to purchase a car. The plaintiff may allege that the defendant wrongfully possesses property owned by the plaintiff. The plaintiff may claim that the defendant has failed to comply with a statute or regulation. Or, the plaintiff may seek a divorce from the defendant.

Many lawsuits allege that the defendant has committed a "tort," a subject that you will study in your first year. A tort is a civil wrong that involves injury to the plaintiff's person or property. Such injuries may occur when the defendant is negligent in causing an automobile accident or in creating some dangerous condition, or commits medical or legal malpractice. Other tort wrongs include manufacturing a defective product, committing defamation, or engaging in certain harmful intentional conduct such as assault or battery, trespass, fraud, or invasion of privacy. These are just a small sampling of claims that may be asserted in a civil lawsuit.

[2] Criminal Cases

Criminal cases are different than civil cases. Criminal cases are not brought by private individuals. Instead, in a criminal case, a government prosecutor (variously referred to as "the United States," "the State," "the prosecution," "the People," or "the

Government") files criminal "charges" against the defendant. Those charges allege that the defendant has committed a particular crime. Although the practice varies by jurisdiction, charges for more serious crimes (like "felonies") often are brought by filing an "indictment."

An indictment is issued by a group of citizens who have been selected to serve on a grand jury. The grand jury issues an indictment upon a finding of "probable cause" (i.e., a reasonable basis to believe) that the defendant may have committed a specified crime. Charges for less serious crimes (like "misdemeanors") often are brought by filing an "information" or a "criminal complaint." An information or complaint is issued by the prosecutor without the involvement of a grand jury, and it sets out the criminal conduct allegedly committed by the defendant. In criminal cases, the "relief" being sought by the prosecuting authority is generally incarceration, probation, and/or a fine.

3.02 The Federal and State Court Systems

In the United States, we have two court systems: the federal courts and the state courts. Civil and criminal cases are heard in either federal or state court, depending upon which court system has authority or "jurisdiction" to decide the particular case.

Generally, federal courts have jurisdiction over a more narrow category of cases than state courts. More specifically, federal courts hear cases involving disputes based on the federal law of the United States or between parties from different states when damages are claimed in excess of a certain amount of money. State courts generally have jurisdiction over disputes between residents of the same state and matters of purely state law based on the state's common law, constitution, statutes, rules or regulations, or ordinances of cities or counties within the state. In some instances, both the state and federal courts may simultaneously have jurisdiction. When that occurs, the plaintiff may choose to bring the case in federal or state court.

[1] The Federal Court System

When a civil or criminal case is brought in the federal court system, the case is usually filed in the "United States District Court," otherwise called the "federal district court." The United States District Court is the federal "trial court" where a single judge, called a "United States District Court Judge," presides. Certain categories of federal cases are heard initially in specialized courts instead of United States District Courts. For example, bankruptcy cases are heard in the "United States Bankruptcy Court," and tax cases are heard in the "United States Tax Court."

Cases in federal district court are typically tried before a jury, with the federal district court judge presiding over the trial. In some cases, the federal district court judge will decide the case alone without a jury. This is called a "bench trial." Regardless of whether the case is ultimately resolved by way of a jury or bench trial, the judge may make various rulings in the case before, during, or after trial. These rulings may deal with matters such as whether particular testimony or exhibits are admissible at trial or whether there is enough evidence for the case to go to trial. Oftentimes, these rulings by the trial judge will be issued in "Memorandum Opinions" or "Orders" that are published and thus become case law.

The party who loses in the federal district court may appeal to the federal appellate court. The federal appellate courts are called the "United States Court of Appeals." The United States Court of Appeals typically hears cases in three judge panels. The United States Court of Appeals is divided into twelve regional "Circuits," with each circuit having appellate jurisdiction over cases decided by the United States District Courts located in a particular area of the country. For example, appeals from the

U.S. District Courts located in Maryland, North Carolina, South
Carolina, Virginia, and West Virginia are filed with the "United
States Court of Appeals for the Fourth Circuit," otherwise simply
called "the Fourth Circuit." The "United States Court of Appeals
for the D.C. Circuit" is unnumbered. In addition, the "United
States Court of Appeals for the Federal Circuit" has nationwide
jurisdiction to hear appeals in certain specialized cases. The following map shows the federal circuits:

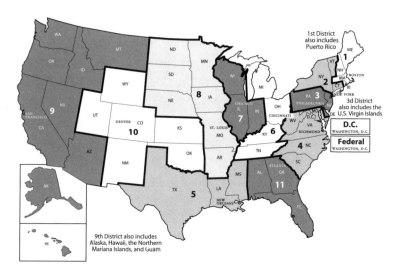

When a case is appealed, there is not a new trial in the appellate court. Instead, the appellate court's job is limited to determining whether, based on the contentions of the appealing
party (the "appellant"), the trial court judge made one or more
legal "errors" during the case. These errors may occur in connection with any of the pretrial or trial procedures discussed in
Section 3.03 below. To aid the appellate court in this task, the
appellant's lawyer and the lawyer for the opposing party (the
"appellee") submit extensive written "briefs" to the appellate
court. Those briefs, which are arguments about the law and its
application to the facts in the case, address the errors that the

appellant contends were made by the trial court judge. The lawyers for both the appellant and the appellee typically will also make an oral argument to the appellate court on these matters. Unlike a trial, no witnesses are called and no evidence is presented during an appellate oral argument. Rather, at oral argument, the lawyers present their contentions to the appellate court judges, who ask the lawyers probing questions about their contentions.

After reviewing the briefs and hearing oral arguments, the appellate court will issue its decision in the case. The decision will either "affirm" by upholding the district court judge's rulings, "reverse" by setting aside or "vacating" those rulings, "modify" those rulings in some way, or "remand" the case back to the district court judge to conduct a new trial or take some other action in the case.

The party who loses at the United States Court of Appeals may ask, through a "Petition for Writ of Certiorari," that the nine justices of the Supreme Court of the United States hear the case. There is, however, rarely an absolute right to have the Supreme Court hear an appeal. With limited exceptions set forth in the U.S. Constitution, the Supreme Court has complete discretion over which cases it considers of sufficient importance to review. The Supreme Court typically agrees to hear approximately 100 cases per year out of thousands of petitions seeking review.

If the Supreme Court accepts review of a case, the process of submitting briefs and making oral arguments takes place again in the Supreme Court. The Supreme Court also has authority in certain circumstances to review a decision of the highest court in a state on a matter involving a question under the U.S. Constitution or a federal statute or federal regulation. The Supreme Court's ultimate decision or opinion in the case will be published and become part of established case law. As the Supreme Court of the United States is the highest court in the land, its opinions trump all other court decisions.

[2] The State Court System

State court systems resemble the federal court system in many ways. But, the names given to particular state trial courts and appellate courts differ from the names given to those courts in the federal system and in other states. Civil and criminal cases brought in state court are initially filed in a trial court, variously called a district court, circuit court, court of common pleas, or superior court. A single judge presides.

Most states have at least one intermediate appellate court (e.g., the Iowa Court of Appeals, or the Oregon Court of Appeals). Some larger states have several intermediate appellate court "divisions," whose jurisdiction is defined geographically much as in the federal system. Cases appealed to these intermediate appellate courts are decided by panels of an odd number of judges, typically three. All states have an appellate court of last resort, which is the highest appellate court in the state. In most states, this court is called the State Supreme Court (although New York, for example, calls it the "Court of Appeals"). Cases heard by the state's highest court are decided by five, seven, or nine justices depending on the state.

The appellate process in state intermediate appellate courts and appellate courts of last resort is generally similar to the federal appellate process described above. Also, similar to the federal appellate process, a state appellate court decision may be published and have precedential value. In some states, certain decisions of trial court judges are published.

[3] Diagram Summarizing Appeals in the Federal and State Court Systems

The following diagram shows the path of a case from the trial court through the appellate courts in the federal and state court systems:

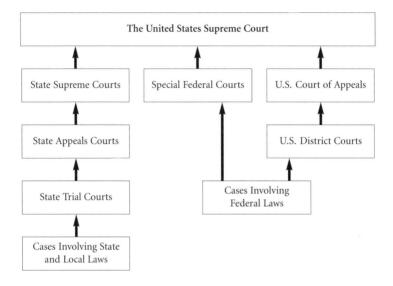

3.03 Pretrial and Trial Procedures for Civil and Criminal Cases

Pretrial and trial procedures are similar in federal and state trial courts; and the conduct of a trial is, to a large extent, similar in civil and criminal cases. In civil cases, pretrial and trial procedures in the U.S. District Court (federal district court) are governed by the Federal Rules of Civil Procedure and certain administrative rules of local district courts. In state civil cases, the pretrial and trial procedures are governed by state rules of civil procedure. In criminal cases, pretrial and trial procedures in the U.S. District Court are governed by the Federal Rules of Criminal Procedure. In state criminal cases, the pretrial and trial procedures are governed by separate state rules of criminal procedure.

Below is a summary of these procedures in the order in which they occur for both the federal and state court systems together.

[1] Civil Cases

(a) The Filing of Pleadings

When a plaintiff begins a lawsuit by filing a Complaint (or Petition) with the trial court, the Complaint will allege (a) the facts of the dispute or the wrongs committed by the defendant, and (b) the legal claims on which the plaintiff is requesting relief from the court. The Complaint must be "served" on the defendant, usually by registered or certified mail or by personal delivery to the defendant.

The defendant will file an "Answer" to the Complaint with the trial court and "serve" the Answer by mailing it to the plaintiff's attorney. The Answer will "admit" the factual allegations in the Complaint that the defendant deems true and "deny" those that the defendant deems false. The Answer will include any special legal "defenses" that the defendant may have to the suit. If a defendant fails to file an Answer to a Complaint, the trial court will grant a "default judgment." In other words, if the defendant fails to file an Answer, then the plaintiff wins.

Sometimes, a defendant may allege in an Answer one or more "counterclaims" against the plaintiff. A counterclaim is the defendant's counter-suit against the plaintiff, and it is the functional equivalent of a plaintiff's Complaint. If a counterclaim is asserted, the plaintiff will file with the court and serve upon the defendant a "Reply" to the counterclaim. This Reply, which is similar to an Answer to a Complaint, will admit or deny the factual allegations asserted in the defendant's counterclaim. The Complaint, Answer, and Reply to a counterclaim are referred to as the "pleadings" in the case.

(b) Pretrial Motions to Dismiss

A "motion" is a request that the court act in a certain way. If the defendant believes that the Complaint is defective in some legal respect, the defendant may file a "Motion to Dismiss" the Complaint. For example, a "Motion to Dismiss for Failure to State a Claim upon Which Relief Can be Granted" may be filed when the facts alleged in the Complaint show that the plaintiff has no claim recognized by the law. For instance, such a motion will be granted if the facts in the Complaint show that it was not filed within the "statute of limitations" — the time frame prescribed by the law for filing the suit. A motion to dismiss might also be granted if the court has no jurisdiction over the case or the parties to the suit.

After the motion is filed, the court may conduct a hearing to consider the attorneys' arguments on the matter. If the court grants the motion to dismiss, the case ends and the losing party's remedy is to appeal the decision. If the court denies the motion, the case moves forward. Generally, there is no immediate right of appeal from the denial of motions to dismiss because appellate courts prefer to consider that issue only after there is a final judgment in the case.

(c) The Discovery Stage

If no immediate motion to dismiss is made or the court denies such a motion, the case proceeds to the "discovery" stage. Discovery is a process by which each side may obtain information from the other about the facts of the case and each side's contentions about those facts. This information may be obtained in a variety of different ways. There are three ways that parties will generally obtain information in written format from the other side.

First, there are "interrogatories," which are written questions sent by one party to the other about the facts of the case. Second, there are written "requests for the production of documents." These essentially require the other side to provide documents that relate to the subject matter of the lawsuit. Third, there are written "requests for admissions." These are requests that ask the other side to agree that certain facts are true. Each side that receives such discovery requests must reply in writing and must make a good faith effort to answer the request.

The discovery process also allows each party to obtain information through in-person interviews of the other party or of witnesses who may have information about the dispute. These interviews are known as "depositions." At a deposition, the lawyer for the party taking the deposition will ask questions of the "deponent" (i.e., the person being deposed). Those questions will focus on the facts of the case or the witness's likely trial testimony. The lawyer for the other party will also have the opportunity to ask questions. This deposition testimony is taken under oath and is recorded and transcribed word-for-word by a "court reporter." The court reporter provides a transcript of the deposition to each lawyer. In some cases, depositions may be taken by video.

The discovery stage may take six months in simpler cases or more than a year in complex cases, and the timetable for completing discovery is typically set by local court rules or by the judge. The basic objective of the process is to allow each party to discover, in advance of trial, the testimony and other evidence that another party may introduce at trial. Discovery also gives the parties a way to learn of information that supports or contradicts the claims and defenses raised in the lawsuit. Any disputes that arise during the discovery process will be resolved by the trial judge.

(d) Motion for Summary Judgment

Early in your law school career, you will read cases dealing with a motion for "summary judgment." This is a common and important procedural motion in civil lawsuits. A motion for summary judgment is sometimes filed after the discovery process has been completed.

In a motion for summary judgment, the party filing the motion contends that the court should decide the case without a trial because the key facts (i.e., the "material facts") in the case are not in dispute. If there are no disputed facts, then there is no need for a jury to decide the case because the sole function of a jury is to resolve the differences about the parties' different versions of the facts. In these circumstances, because the judge is the only person who is empowered to decide the law that is applicable to the case, the party moving for summary judgment asks the judge to go ahead and decide the case in that party's favor "as a matter of law" in light of the undisputed facts.

When such a motion is filed, the judge may conduct a hearing to consider the arguments of counsel. The judge will also review the facts and evidence submitted by the parties based on the discovery in the case. Summary judgment will be granted only if the judge concludes that: (1) viewing the facts in a light most favorable to the party opposing the motion, there are no genuine issues of material fact in the case; and (2) the party making the motion is entitled to a judgment in that party's favor under the law. If the motion is granted, the losing party's remedy is to appeal the ruling. If the motion is denied, the case proceeds to trial. Many civil cases are resolved by summary judgment rather than by trial.

(e) The Jury Trial

A jury trial consists of the ten basic stages summarized below.

(1)   Jury Selection. A jury (usually consisting of twelve people) is selected through a process by which the judge, and often the lawyers, question potential jurors about matters bearing upon their ability to decide the case fairly and impartially. The lawyers have the right to excuse a certain number of potential jurors for virtually any reason, except for certain classifications such as race or gender. In addition, the judge has the authority to excuse any potential juror that the judge believes will not be fair and impartial in the case.

(2) Opening Statements. Each side has an opportunity to make an "opening statement" to the jury. These opening statements are merely a "forecast" of the evidence that each side intends to present, and arguments about the evidence are prohibited. Usually, the plaintiff's lawyer gives an opening statement first, followed by the opening statement of the defendant's lawyer.

(3) Plaintiff's Presentation of Evidence. The plaintiff presents evidence first. The presentation of evidence consists of the testimony of witnesses and the introduction of exhibits. The plaintiff's witnesses will first testify on "direct" examination in response to questions asked by the plaintiff's lawyer. The defendant's lawyer then has the right to "cross-examine" each of the plaintiff's witnesses after they testify on direct examination.

All objections to the admissibility of testimony and exhibits are decided by the judge. A judge rules on an objection by either agreeing with the attorney who objected to the evidence, or by disagreeing with the attorney's objection. If the judge agrees, he will respond with "sustained"; if the judge disagrees, finding the evidence admissible, he will respond with "overruled."

(4) Motion for Directed Verdict. After all of the plaintiff's witnesses have testified and exhibits have been received into evidence, the plaintiff's "case-in-chief" is complete. At this point, the defendant's lawyer may make an oral motion to the judge (outside the presence of the jury) for a "directed verdict." The judge will grant this motion if, viewing the evidence in the light most favorable to the plaintiff, no reasonable juror could find in favor of the plaintiff. The judge may also grant this motion when a judgment against the plaintiff is otherwise compelled by the law based on the evidence presented. If a directed verdict motion is granted, the case is dismissed, and the plaintiff's remedy is to file an appeal. If the motion is denied, the trial continues.

(5) The Defendant's Evidence. The defendant will then have the opportunity to call witnesses to testify and introduce exhibits.

The defendant presents evidence following the same order and process as the plaintiff. Because the defendant is now calling witnesses and introducing evidence, the plaintiff's lawyer has the right to cross-examine the defendant's witnesses. When the defendant has finished presenting testimony and exhibits, the defendant's case-in-chief is complete. At this point, the defendant will usually renew the earlier motion for a directed verdict. If the motion is granted, the case ends; if it is denied, the case continues.

(6)   Rebuttal Evidence. The plaintiff will have the opportunity to introduce "rebuttal" evidence. Rebuttal evidence is limited to evidence that counters the evidence the defendant presented. If the plaintiff introduces rebuttal evidence, then the defendant may have an opportunity to introduce "surrebuttal" evidence. The limitations upon the defendant in presenting surrebuttal evidence are similar to the limitations placed upon the plaintiff in presenting rebuttal evidence—i.e., the defendant is limited to presenting evidence that counters the plaintiff's rebuttal evidence. After this additional evidence is presented by the attorneys and received by the court, both sides "rest," meaning that the evidentiary phase of the trial is over.

(7)   The Jury Charge Conference. After the parties have rested, the judge will hold a "jury charge" or "jury instruction" conference with the parties' lawyers (outside the presence of the jury). During that conference, the judge and lawyers will discuss the specific jury instructions that the judge intends to give the jury before it deliberates. These instructions, which are carefully written to be read to the jury by the judge, serve two purposes. First, they set out the specific "issues" or questions that the jury must answer by completing a "Verdict Form." Second, they explain the pertinent law regarding those issues or questions. The jury will be required to apply the pertinent law to the evidence that was presented during the trial. The lawyers are entitled both to object to any of the proposed instructions and to propose alter-

native instructions. The judge will rule on those objections and proposed alternative instructions. The judge will then finalize the instructions and read them aloud to the jury after closing arguments.

(8)   Closing Arguments. The lawyers for the parties will make closing arguments to the jury. Closing arguments are designed to persuade the jurors to reach a particular verdict. In a civil case, the plaintiff bears the burden of proving the case usually by a "preponderance of the evidence" (i.e., the greater weight of the evidence). There are certain cases, however, where "clear and convincing evidence" is required. Because the plaintiff bears the burden of proof, the plaintiff's lawyer usually has the right to make the first and last closing argument. Thus, the plaintiff's lawyer will argue first, followed by the defense lawyer's argument, and finally the plaintiff's lawyer will have the opportunity to respond to defense counsel's argument.

(9)   The Jury Charge. The judge will "charge" the jury by reading the final jury instructions and explaining the jury verdict form. For example, if the plaintiff is seeking money damages for injuries sustained in an automobile accident allegedly caused by the defendant, the issues on the verdict form to be decided by the jury might be: "(1) Was the defendant negligent in causing the automobile accident? (2) If 'yes,' was the defendant's negligence the proximate cause of the plaintiff's injuries? (3) If 'yes,' what amount of damages is the plaintiff entitled to recover from the defendant?" In connection with these issues, the judge will explain to the jury the law about "negligence," "proximate cause," and "damages." The judge will also give special instructions about the burden of proof and other matters pertaining to the evidence received in the case.

(10)   Jury Deliberation and Verdict. After reading the jury instructions, the judge will send the jury to the jury room to deliberate behind closed doors. When the jury informs the judge that it has reached a verdict, which usually must be unanimous,

the judge will bring the jury back into the courtroom to announce the verdict and to enter a final judgment. Following rulings on any post-trial motions, the losing party's remedy is to appeal the final judgment.

[2] Criminal Cases

(a) Pretrial Proceedings

The Fourth Amendment to the U.S. Constitution requires that when a law enforcement officer arrests a person, the arrest must be supported by "probable cause" that the person has committed a crime. There are two different types of arrests: (1) arrests made with an arrest warrant; and (2) arrests made without an arrest warrant. When an arrest is made with an arrest warrant, probable cause for the arrest has already been determined by a judge.

When an officer arrests a suspect without first obtaining a warrant, the court must determine whether there was probable cause for the officer to have made the arrest. Thus, usually within twenty-four hours after arrest, the arrestee is taken before a judge for a "first appearance" (otherwise called an initial appearance, an initial arraignment, arraignment on a warrant, or arraignment on a complaint). At the first appearance, the judge will determine if the police had probable cause to make the arrest. In many jurisdictions, the judge will also inform the arrestee of the charges, advise the arrestee of the right to counsel, the privilege against self-incrimination, and the right to trial by jury. If the arrestee is unable to afford a lawyer, the court may appoint a defense lawyer to represent the arrestee. Additionally, the judge will determine whether the arrestee should be set free on his or her own recognizance, released on bail, or detained pending further proceedings. The judge will then set a date for a "preliminary hearing."

A "preliminary hearing" is a type of mini-trial where the judge (without a jury) must determine whether to continue to hold the arrestee for further proceedings. The preliminary hearing is designed to determine whether there is sufficient evidence to permit a trial of the accused. The preliminary hearing is used in more than half of the states, usually as an alternative to the determination of probable cause by a grand jury issuing an indictment. In federal court, however, the Constitution requires that an accused be charged with a felony by way of grand jury indictment.

During the preliminary hearing, the prosecution must merely produce sufficient evidence to convince the judge that there is probable cause to believe that the accused may be guilty of the crime charged. At this stage, the prosecution does not have to prove that the accused is guilty beyond a reasonable doubt. The accused is entitled to be present at the hearing, to be represented by counsel, to cross-examine the prosecution's witnesses, and to introduce evidence. If the judge does not find probable cause, the case is dismissed. If the judge finds probable cause, the case will proceed to trial.

After the preliminary hearing, the official charges against the defendant will be filed in the form of either an information prepared by the prosecutor or an indictment issued by a grand jury. The information or indictment will be formally presented to the defendant at a court proceeding called an "arraignment." At an arraignment, the defendant will enter a plea of either "not guilty," "guilty," or "*nolo contendere.*" A "*nolo contendere*" plea means "I will not contest the charges," and it is essentially treated the same as a guilty plea.

(b) Pretrial Motions

After the arraignment, defendants often make various pretrial motions. These motions may challenge the charges on various technical grounds or contend that certain evidence should be "suppressed" (or excluded) from trial because it was obtained in violation of the Constitution. In some circumstances, if a defendant's pretrial motions are successful, the judge will dismiss the charges. Absent a dismissal, the case moves forward to trial.

(c) The Limited Discovery Process

The discovery process in criminal cases is different — and more limited — than in civil cases. The parties in criminal cases do not use the discovery methods available in civil cases. Instead, the applicable statutory rules of criminal procedure specify the information that each party must provide to the other in advance of trial. This information usually includes written statements of the accused and of witnesses, summaries of expert reports, and certain exhibits that may be used in the case.

(d) The Jury Trial

In a criminal case, the basic stages of a jury trial are very similar to those in a civil trial. In a criminal case, however, the prosecutor occupies the position of the plaintiff's lawyer in a civil case. In other words, the prosecutor bears the burden of proof in the case, makes the first opening statement, presents evidence first, and has the right to make the last closing argument. Unlike a civil case where the burden of proof is typically "preponderance of the evidence," in a criminal case the prosecutor bears the burden of proving guilt "beyond a reasonable doubt." That is the highest burden of proof recognized by our legal system.

Like a motion for a directed verdict in a civil case, at the end of the prosecution's case-in-chief, a criminal defense lawyer may make a motion for "judgment of acquittal." A judge will grant a motion for judgment of acquittal only if, viewing the evidence in the light most favorable to the prosecution, no reasonable juror could find the defendant guilty beyond a reasonable doubt.

If the judge grants the motion for judgment of acquittal, the case is over. If the judge denies the motion for judgment of acquittal, the case proceeds and the defense may present evidence. In criminal trials, the defendant cannot be forced to testify. That is so because of the Fifth Amendment right against self-incrimination.

(e) The Sentencing Process

If the defendant is convicted at trial, the judge usually conducts sentencing at a later hearing without a jury. At the sentencing hearing, the lawyers will present arguments on what they believe should be an appropriate sentence. The judge will consider those arguments, along with the statements of any victims or other witnesses who may wish to testify at the sentencing hearing. The defendant also has a right to address the judge in "allocution" prior to the imposition of sentencing. After considering all of that information, the judge will impose a sentence within the parameters allowed by the law.

(f) Appeals

If the defendant is acquitted (i.e., found not guilty) by the jury or by the judge, the prosecution is barred by the Double Jeopardy Clause of the U.S. Constitution from appealing the acquittal. However, if the prosecutor disagrees with the sentence imposed upon the defendant after conviction, the prosecution may appeal the judge's sentencing order. If the defendant is convicted, he has a statutory right to appeal the conviction and sentence.

After a defendant has exhausted all appeals, he or she may seek additional review of the conviction and sentence by filing a "Petition for Writ of *Habeas Corpus*" in a federal district court. Such a petition will only be granted if the defendant can establish that his or her continued incarceration would violate the U.S. Constitution or federal law.

[3] Diagram Summarizing Pretrial and Trial Procedures

Pretrial and Trial Procedures — in Chronological Order	
Civil Cases	**Criminal Cases**
Filing of pleadings	Pretrial proceedings
Pretrial motions to dismiss	Pretrial motions
The discovery stage	The limited discovery process
Motion for summary judgment	The jury trial
The jury trial	The sentencing process
Appeals	Appeals

Ten Basic Stages of a Jury Trial

1. Jury Selection
2. Opening Statements
3. The Plaintiff's/Prosecution's Evidence
4. Motions to Dismiss
5. The Defendant's Evidence
6. Rebuttal evidence
7. Jury Charge Conference
8. Closing Arguments
9. The Jury Charge
10. Jury Deliberation and Verdict

No doubt this chapter has been difficult to read. Even if it felt like slogging through mud, you were learning a critical framework for studying the law. You will want to refer back to this chapter during the first few weeks and months of law school.

Chapter 4

How to Study Law — The Basics

Synopsis

The law is not the place for the artist or the poet. The law is the calling of thinkers.

— Oliver Wendell Holmes

The preceding chapters of this book set the stage for what you will be studying in law school. This chapter provides general guidance about how to study in your first year. If you follow it closely, you will know how to approach your studies and what to expect on your first day of classes. Later chapters of this book will provide further explanation and additional examples about the topics introduced in this chapter — i.e., how to read and brief cases through the case-law method of learning law, how to participate in class, how to prepare course outlines, how to use common sense when thinking about the law, some pointers about legal research and writing, and how to study for and take law school exams.

4.01 Reading Slowly

For starters, read this chapter *slowly*. Notice the italics? Don't skim or skipp through the chapter. Did you notice the word that was misspelled in the previous sentence? You should have—and will—only if you read slowly, word for word. When studying law, you need to get used to reading slowly.

This is important because words matter in the law. The precise meaning of the law depends largely on the particular words used. As a result, studying in law school is quite different from studying in undergraduate school.

In undergraduate school, many students "study" by simply skimming the chapter in their textbook to get the "gist" or main ideas of the chapter. This study approach doesn't work in law school. Let us say it again—this study approach doesn't work in law school. Learning the law often requires you to recognize and understand subtle distinctions in the particular words used in the law. For example, the difference between the words "may" and "shall" is critical, as the former speaks permissively while the latter speaks mandatorily.

The actual language of the law carries real-life consequences. One word in a contract or a statute just might determine who will win or lose a case or what decision a client should make about a particular matter. Your clients will be depending on *you* to catch that one word. Indeed, there are cases that have been won or lost based entirely on the way in which a common word was used in a piece of legislation or in a legal document. Thus, whenever you read a case decision, constitutional provision, statute, or a rule or regulation, read slowly. Read each and every word. When studying the law, there is no such thing as

"TL;DR"—"Too Long; Didn't Read." There are no shortcuts. You must read thoroughly. You must read slowly.

4.02 What Law School Teaches

Law school teaches you the basic skills necessary to be a lawyer. More specifically, you will learn to: (1) research the pertinent law; (2) understand the law; (3) apply the law to particular factual situations; (4) advise your client about the best decision to make or the best way to resolve the problem; (5) communicate effectively, both orally and in writing; and (6) advocate for your client.

But, most importantly, law school teaches you "how to think like a lawyer." This commonly used phrase, which by itself explains little, refers to a disciplined form of thinking that is necessary to solve both legal and non-legal problems. This type of thinking involves: (1) obtaining all of the relevant facts of the particular situation; (2) identifying the legal (and sometimes non-legal) principles that are pertinent to the situation; and (3) applying those principles to the relevant facts to determine what best to do about the situation. This careful form of thinking is commonly referred to as "legal analysis" or "legal reasoning," and it is embodied within every case decision you will read. You will soon discover that case decisions follow a uniform structure that contains: (1) the facts of the case and its procedural history; (2) the pertinent law; (3) the application of the law to the facts; and (4) the ultimate decision or result in the case.

You will be required to engage in this type of thinking from the first day of law school through the last day. Your professors will call on you and ask: "Ms. Smith, what are the facts of *Jones v. Doe*?" or "Mr. Bobbit, what rule did the court apply to resolve the dispute between the parties?" At first, you will likely experience some difficulty answering because learning to think in this way is a foreign concept. Indeed, learning the language of the law is, itself, much like learning a foreign language.

Rest assured, with time and diligent study you will become accustomed to this way of thinking. You will become an expert problem solver. In the end, and with additional experience in practice, you will have the intellectual ability to effectively advise and represent not only the client who may be deciding whether and how to distribute her property in a will, but even the President of the United States who may be deciding whether and how to conduct a war. (If the latter assertion sounds too hyperbolic, you may want to read *The Iraq Study Group Report*, which was written in 2006 by ten prominent presidential appointees—eight of whom were lawyers—to advise the President about how to best address the continuing U.S. military strategy in Iraq).

Now re-read—slowly—the last three paragraphs. They are critically important to your success as a law student.

4.03 The Case-Law Method of Learning the Law

In your first year, you will be enrolled in "doctrinal-law" courses, e.g. *Civil Procedure, Contracts, Constitutional Law, Torts, Property*, and *Criminal Law*. In addition, you will be exposed to *Legal Research* and *Legal Writing*. In your second and third years, you will have other courses in doctrinal law and legal writing. You will also have a broad choice of various "elective" courses in different areas of the law, and you will have the opportunity to take "practical-skills" courses or clinical programs.

Each of your first-year doctrinal-law courses will seem like a separate, foreign language. Little, if anything, of what you studied in undergraduate school or any graduate school will give you an advantage in these courses. This is what makes them difficult. Their content and language will be totally unfamiliar.

This means that, particularly in your first semester, much of what you study and hear in the classroom may seem like "Greek," so to speak. But, that is no cause to be alarmed. From the beginning, expect this strangeness, accept it, and embrace it as something that is entirely normal not only for you, but also for your fellow students. Be patient with yourself, which means have some humility. You *will* "get it" if you give the learning process its due time and effort.

Your professors will have different styles, and they will use various methods to teach these first-year doctrinal-law courses. Typically, however, you will be reading from a book that contains actual case decisions written by appellate court judges or justices. This method of learning the law by studying "case law" is designed to: (1) repeatedly expose you to the structure of legal thinking or analysis described above; (2) provide you with the particular principles of law that pertain to the dispute between the parties in the case; and (3) enable you to see how the court applies the applicable principles of law to the particular facts of the case to reach a decision. The overall goal of the case method of instruction is that you will learn the law and how to conduct legal analysis by seeing how the courts apply the law to different factual situations.

Consider an example of this from a *Contracts* course. When a lawyer is confronted with a dispute involving an alleged breach of contract, the lawyer will typically analyze the following preliminary questions: (1) was there a valid contract?; (2) if so, was there a breach or violation of the contract?; (3) if there was a breach, what rights or remedies are available to the non-breaching party?; and (4) does the breaching party have any defenses?

A typical law school casebook on *Contracts* will contain case decisions that address the first question—i.e., the legal principles (or legal "elements") of a valid contract. You will learn that an enforceable express contract basically requires all of the following: (a) a valid "offer," (b) valid "acceptance" of the offer, and (c) valid "consideration" for the contract (i.e., an exchange of legitimate promises or commitments between the parties). The casebook might begin in the first chapter with case decisions about what constitutes a valid offer, followed by cases dealing with valid acceptance, and then with valid consideration. By reading these cases, you will learn the law about each of these requirements and how they are satisfied based on the facts of particular cases. Then, in later chapters, the text will likely turn to cases that deal with the questions of breach of contract and remedies for and defenses to a breach.

Be aware, however, that reading case decisions in a casebook is not like reading an undergraduate textbook. Your casebook will rarely have bullet points or charts or pictures that explain to you what the court is doing and why. It will be *your* job to read the cases and to discern the applicable principles for *yourself*.

So, how do you do that? What do you do when reading these cases? First, remember to read each case *very slowly*. If you don't know the meaning of a word, legal or not, look it up. Yes, we mean actually go on the Internet or, preferably, pick up the dictionary (a "legal dictionary") and look up the definition of the word. This is absolutely essential for learning the language and meaning of the law.

When reading a case, you need to be *actively* reading. This means that as you are reading the case, you should underline or "highlight" the following:

(1) the key *facts* of the case, including what happened in the lower courts (i.e., its procedural history);
(2) the precise *issue* or question in the case that the court is deciding;
(3) the key *principles of law* stated by the court;
(4) the critical aspects of *the court's application* of the legal principles to the particular facts; and
(5) the bottom-line decision or *result* in the case.

Underline in such a way that, from the particular words and phrases you underline, you can articulate in class each of these components just by "glancing" at your underlining. You might start out using a pencil with a good eraser because you will tend to underline too much at first. If you notice this happening, go back and erase all but the essential language. In the margin of the case, you should identify in handwriting those parts of your underlining that correspond to components (1) through (5) above and make any notes or questions you have about the case. (Chapter 5 of this book explains more about how to actively read cases through the underlining method).

Some may suggest that you highlight by "color coding" the different components of a case (e.g., yellow for the "facts," red for the "issue," green for the "law," blue for the Court's "application of the law to the facts," and purple or some other color for the "result"). Some students find this technique useful, but others find it cumbersome or messy; and lawyers in actual practice do not usually use it. Careful and selective underlining will do the job just fine.

In addition, you will have to learn how to write a "case brief," which is a summary of the key information found in a case decision. A case brief is a document you create, and it is your written summary of: (1) the facts and procedural history of the case decision; (2) the issue and holding in the case; (3) the rules of law stated by the court; (4) the court's application of the law to the facts; and (5) the result in the case. (Chapter 6 of this book further explains and provides examples of how to write a case brief).

For law school, reading case decisions effectively and writing case briefs are essential for proper class preparation and for learning the course material. (See Chapter 7 of this book about class preparation and how to participate in class.) Additionally, these skills are important for preparing a "Detailed Course Outline of the Law," which is introduced below.

4.04 Preparing a Detailed Course Outline of the Law

At the end of your first semester of law school, you will need to know and understand the law in each course. You will also need to know how to apply the law to new fact patterns. In fact, you will be tested on your knowledge of the law and its application to different facts by one or more exams. (See Chapter 11 of this book on "How to Study for Exams & Write Law School Exam Answers.") Unlike undergraduate school—where you may have studied for an exam by cramming all of the information into your head the week before an exam—in law school you *must* be studying for exams *throughout* the entire semester. How do you do that?

To begin with, you will not know in advance the questions on the exam. Your professors will not give you a study guide. Due to practical time constraints, your exams certainly will not cover everything in the course. But, your professors will assume you have prepared for the exam by learning *all* of the law in the course. Thus, your preparation for exams must embrace a thorough understanding of the law and its application in *all* areas covered in the course.

This preparation should begin *within the first two weeks* of class. And, it must continue throughout the semester. Attempting to "cram" in law school will be fatal. You must pace yourself and regularly review material, even as you read cases for the next day's classes. Is this difficult? Yes. Will it prepare you to succeed? Yes.

For each topic of law covered in a course, you should prepare a detailed course outline of the law on that topic and its application in the course. This detailed course outline, *in the precise language of the law,* will be the document that you will review, over and over again, in preparation for your exam. Put simply, you can't succeed in law school without detailed course outlines.

This detailed course outline must contain (1) *precise and accurate* statements of the legal principles, and (2) notes of examples about how those legal principles apply to different factual circumstances. Your outline must be prepared based on *your* careful reading of the case decisions in your book, *your* case briefs on those decisions, and *your* class notes.

For example, assume that in a *Contracts* course the topic is, as introduced above, the elements of an enforceable express contract. As previously stated, generally this requires (a) a valid offer, (b) a valid acceptance, and (c) valid consideration. Your detailed course outline of the requirement of a "valid offer" might be as follows:

I. Valid Offer

A. An offer is an unequivocal statement of a commitment to be bound. A mere "preliminary negotiation," "invitation to bargain," advertisement, price quotation, or joke is not an offer capable of acceptance.

B. The language of the offer—sometimes considering the surrounding circumstances, previous communications between the parties, or industry custom—must be:

1. unequivocal, and

2. reasonably definite in its terms (i.e., price, quantity, and time of performance) or capable of being made definite by the court to provide a remedy.

E.g., language such as "*might* be willing; will *consider*; *not possible unless* I receive $$; we are *authorized* to offer; we *intend* to pay" is too equivocal. This language is not "an unequivocal statement of a commitment to be bound."

C. The offer must be communicated, and may be oral unless a writing is required under the Statute of Frauds....

Your outline should be written *by you alone*. Sometimes, students try to team up with one another to prepare a group outline. Or, even worse, students will purchase a commercially produced outline of the course. Neither practice is useful because an outline written by a group of students or by a commercial enterprise is unlikely to be easily understood by you for one simple reason — you didn't write it. To be as effective as possible, the outline must be generated from *your own* understanding of the law so that *you* can apply it on an exam.

There is, however, one situation in which a commercial product may be of assistance to you. As you prepare your outlines (or if you are confused by a particular case or topic discussed in class), you may find it helpful to consult books that are known as "treatises" or "hornbooks." These are books authored by law professors and written for law students to help them understand the doctrinal law on a particular subject. There are a variety of different treatises and hornbooks on each topic you will study in law school. You should consult your syllabus, as your professor may recommend a particular treatise or hornbook. You also may want to ask your professor what treatise or hornbook he or she might recommend. If your professor recommends a particular hornbook or treatise, then by all means you should follow that recommendation.

If you are searching for a hornbook and your professor has not made a recommendation, you may want to consult the *Understanding* series published by Carolina Academic Press (formerly by LexisNexis). There is an *Understanding* book for each of the subjects typically included within the first year law school curriculum: *Understanding Contracts*, *Understanding Torts*, *Understanding Civil Procedure*, *Understanding Criminal Law*, *Understanding Property*, and *Understanding Constitutional Law*. Students oftentimes find these books very helpful, particularly when they are struggling to understand a particular topic. Some other publishers have similar books on the subjects covered in first year courses, and your library will have many of them on reserve for you to use. However, a note of caution is required here: you should only use treatises and hornbooks as a *supplement* to—and *not* as a substitute for—your casebook, case briefs, and class notes.

As you are preparing your course outline, you should be consulting your casebook, case briefs, class notes, and a hornbook or treatise. Doing so will ensure that you have a comprehensive and accurate outline that will help you to master the particular subject matter. (Chapter 8 of this book further explains how to prepare a detailed course outline.) Remember that you are in control of your own destiny. Outlining is a marathon, not a sprint.

4.05 Handwriting or Typing Course Outlines and Class Notes

Considerable research shows that writing *in longhand* enhances our memory about what we write and makes us more exact about what we write. For this reason, as well as to keep students focused in class, some professors prohibit typing in class altogether. The benefits of writing in longhand suggest that it is best to write course outlines and take class notes by hand. If you take advantage of this writing method, you should keep your outline in a 3-ring, loose-leaf binder so that you can easily add to and rearrange the pages of your outline to optimize its organization. In addition, if you write your outline in pencil rather than pen, you will find it easier to erase and edit what you have written to produce a clean and legible outline.

If you decide to type your outline, carefully guard against being wordy or writing unnecessary material. Your outline must be *exact in stating the law* and provide short and clear examples of *how* the law applies to different factual situations. Freely edit and revise your outline to maximize this exactness. Periodically print out your outline and keep it in a loose-leaf binder. Then you can still draw upon the benefits of handwriting by using longhand to underscore important definitions or points in your outline or to make additional notations in the margins of your outline. Indeed, some students who type their outlines find it beneficial to handwrite a condensed version when studying for exams. In short, you will better understand and remember a typewritten outline if you *actively interact with it* by writing on it in your own handwriting.

4.06 Legal Research and Writing

In many ways, lawyers are professional researchers and writers. It follows, therefore, that to succeed as a lawyer you must learn to research the law and to effectively communicate about the law in writing. Both are difficult at the outset, but you will hone these skills with persistent practice throughout your law school career. All law schools require their first year students to take courses on legal research and writing. At some schools, the two topics are combined into one course. At other schools, the two topics are separated into two distinct courses. Regardless of the format your school has adopted, the advice that follows applies with full force.

Given that quality writing is critical to success as a lawyer, it should come as no surprise to you that *Legal Writing* is the most important course you will take in law school. It is also one of the hardest courses for professors to teach, and it is a class that few students enjoy while they are taking it. Why? Because it's tough. It's not sexy. But, it closely mirrors what you will be doing as an attorney—communicating about a legal issue using the written word. Doing particularly well in your *Legal Writing* course is also a marketable accomplishment you can emphasize to prospective employers because many legal employers want to hire the best writers.

It may be disheartening for some of you to hear, but the fact that you were an English major, a journalist, or the author of a Ph.D. dissertation in graduate school, does not necessarily give you a leg up in your *Legal Writing* course. Legal writing is entirely different from any writing you have done before, and it will take time to learn. This new type of writing is difficult because: (1) its content—the law—is foreign to you; (2) the writing must be structured in the fundamental structure of legal thinking and analysis discussed previously, which is also foreign to you; and (3) the writing must be extremely accurate, precise, and clear to accomplish its real-life objective, which often involves persuasive advocacy of your client's position before a court or other decision-making body.

In addition, learning legal writing is frustrating because its mastery depends primarily upon *your* efforts to completely and repeatedly *re-write* (not merely edit or revise) your writing assignments when the feedback from your professor may be largely negative and instructive in only an abstract way. Contrary to what many students sometimes request of their writing professor, he or she cannot re-write your assignment for you. Instead, you must apply the basic guidance you receive from your professor to re-write your assignment *on your own*. It is through the *re-writing* process that you will become a better writer. (Chapter 10 of this book provides you with some important pointers for writing your first Memorandum of Law.)

The bottom line about legal writing, particularly in the first year, is that you should expect, and therefore embrace as normal, three realities: (1) you will find legal writing difficult and you should be humbled by the learning experience; (2) you will find that doing well in legal writing will require much more time than you anticipated; and (3) with diligence and patience, your writing, including the quality of your legal analysis, will dramatically improve over time. This is a learning process that will extend into your second and third years. Ultimately, your mastery of legal writing will help you not only get a job, but excel in it.

As for *Legal Research*, your first exposure to this skill is likely to be frustrating because the instruction you receive will, at first, appear to be highly abstract; and this type of research will, again, be foreign to you. The key to learning this skill, however, is to "just do it." Literally put your hands on and use the books in the law library. Once you learn where these books are in the library, what they contain, and start actually using them, legal research will become more comprehensible. (Chapter 10 of this book provides you with some additional assistance about conducting legal research *after* you have first learned the basics of legal research from your *Legal Research* course.)

You will also be exposed to online legal research, which is quickly becoming the most prevalent mode of legal research for practicing lawyers. In the long run, online research will make book-oriented law libraries largely obsolete. There are a variety of different online legal research services, such as WestlawNext, Lexis Advance, JustCite, HeinOnline, and Bloomberg Law, among others.

Here are two tips. First, fully learn how to conduct legal research *through the use of the actual books in the law library*. Doing so will enable you to better understand how online legal research works. Additionally, there are times when using the books is actually more efficient than using an online legal research service. Second, become proficient in the use of "West's Topic and Key Number" digest system commonly used for conducting legal research. (See Chapter 10 for more about conducting legal research.)

4.07 Grades

All law students are concerned about law school grades. This is understandable because, to a certain degree, grades are a measure of your performance in law school and will impact your initial marketability for entry-level law positions upon graduation. In the long-run of your career, however, your grades in law school will prove to be much less important than your performance as a lawyer.

Grades in law school—like all grades—are only a partial measure of what you have learned. And, some lower grades will not harm your legal career. Grades do not reflect many quintessential attributes of first-rate lawyering, including sound judgment, the ability to relate to clients and others, and professionalism. In the end, your law school grades, while important, do not and will not ultimately define you as a lawyer in terms of your knowledge of the law, legal skills, or unique ability to contribute through service in the law.

You should know that although grades may be on *your* mind, they are *not* a primary concern of your law professors, except when a particularly low or failing grade may be at issue. Rather, your professors are devoted to your development as a unique person with a unique contribution to others through the law. Your professors want you to grow *into the law*, not only in terms of becoming knowledgeable and keen about what the law means, but how it can be effectively applied by you in your own special way.

If you approach law school with the primary goal of trying to get a certain grade, you risk losing out on the primary mission of your professors and the school as a whole, which is focused on developing you as a professional. Your goal should be to master the material, to immerse yourself in the law, to learn discipline, and to cultivate sound judgment. Oftentimes, but not always, that will translate into a good grade. Law school is certainly not a place where you can receive high grades while putting in minimal effort—a trend that is all too common for some students in undergraduate school. Rather, law school is a place where you are being trained in a noble profession—a calling that does not merely provide you with a livelihood, but with a unique opportunity to serve others. Grades, although important, should not interfere with this overriding perspective.

4.08 Collaboration in Learning the Law and Study Groups

Learning law is not a solitary matter, either in law school or in practice. We learn the law best and, as a result, practice it better when we do so collaboratively. Collaborating with colleagues can be tremendously beneficial and yes, even tremendous fun. It allows you to hash out subtle nuances in the law and discuss and debate varying points of view, and it ensures that you correctly interpreted a judge's opinion—all which are necessary to both higher grades in law school and effective representation in practice. This type of collaboration begins in law school when you interact with both your professors and fellow students.

Some students collaborate by forming study groups of between two and five members. However, a study group is by no means necessary to learning the law; and many students find those groups to be more of a hindrance than a help, if not largely a waste of time. Thus, many students simply draw upon one another on an *ad hoc* basis—whether to discuss some confusing aspect of the law, to share class notes when one of them must miss a class, or sometimes to strategize about how to approach potential exam questions.

On the other hand, some students find that periodic meetings of a study group are helpful if the group has a *clearly focused* agenda—whether to review certain topics of the law previously covered in the course, to discuss specific issues raised in class, or to share questions with one another about matters which members of the group do not understand. A study group, however, is no substitute for preparing your detailed course outlines *on your own*.

In sum, from the first day of law school, you should feel free to reach out and collaborate with your fellow students and faculty. Feel free to be engaged, to interact, to debate, to question, to share, to help, to seek help. Just as the law is an intellectual enterprise, it is also a highly personal and personable enterprise.

Remember that your faculty and fellow students all stand by you—not to sink or swim in this endeavor, but to fully succeed in it, individually and together. (See also Chapter 12 of this book about how to make the most of your first year.)

Chapter 5

How to Read Case Decisions

Synopsis

> *Our opinions are at best provisional hypotheses.*
>
> —*Learned Hand*

Almost all doctrinal-law courses in law school require you to read appellate case decisions published by courts throughout the country. Learning to effectively read case decisions is not only essential for doing well in law school, it is also an indispensable lawyering skill. These case decisions will be reproduced in an edited format in your course text. They will explain the relevant principles of law and apply those principles to the particular facts of disputes being litigated between real-life parties. In other words, the reading of case decisions allows you to see legal analysis in action. This chapter provides you with pointers on how to read case decisions effectively.

5.01 Reading Case Decisions Effectively

Here are seven pointers for reading case decisions effectively:

(1) Start by reading the case all the way through without attempting to underline, highlight, or annotate with notes in the margins. This first read-through is designed to give you a general

sense of what the case is about. It will help you in your selective underlining of the case in the next step. In this first read, you might find it helpful to note some technical items that are part of the case decision.

One of these technical items is the "case caption." Usually, the name that appears first in the caption will be either that of the plaintiff (in a civil case) or the prosecuting government (in a criminal case), and the name that appears second in both civil and criminal cases will be that of the defendant. Most of the case decisions you read will be appellate court decisions, and you should be sure to identify the particular appellate court that rendered the decision (e.g., state or federal intermediate appellate court or supreme court). The name of the appealing party who lost at the trial court level will be designated the "appellant" or "petitioner." The name of the non-appealing party who won at the trial court level will be designated the "appellee" or "respondent."

Particularly when reading U.S. Supreme Court opinions, you should also note the name of the judge who authored the case decision. As explained in Chapter 3, if you are reading an appellate court decision, the case will have been considered by a panel consisting of multiple judges. Many of the case decisions you read in law school will be majority decisions, meaning that a majority of the judges who heard the case agreed with the reasoning and result of the decision. One of the judges who voted with the majority will be assigned the task of writing the "majority opinion." It is oftentimes important for you to know who wrote the majority opinion, because certain judges play important roles in the development of particular areas of law.

At times, especially in *Constitutional Law*, you will read "concurring" or "dissenting" opinions. A concurring opinion is written by a judge who agrees with the ultimate result reached by the majority opinion but who believes the court should have taken a different approach to reach that result. A dissenting opinion is written by a judge who disagrees with the result reached by the majority opinion. Concurring and dissenting opinions are important, because they provide you with an opportunity to understand the arguments on all sides of a particular issue. Additionally, concurring and dissenting opinions are important because, over time, courts may change their earlier rulings and adopt the reasoning contained in prior concurring or dissenting opinions.

(2)   After your first read-through of the case, read it again — this time, *slowly and deliberately*. As part of that slow and deliberate reading, you should selectively underline:

> (a) the key *facts* of the case (including its procedural history);

> (b) the *issue* that the court is deciding;

> (c) the *rules of law* that the court says are applicable to the issue;

> (d) the court's *application of the rules of law to the facts* of the case; and

> (e) the ultimate *result* by the court in the case.

Do this in such a way that, based *solely* on your selective and careful underlining, you can merely glance at that underlining to explain all of (a) through (e). (Chapter 6 provides a detailed discussion that will help you identify the facts, the issue, the rules of law, the application of the rules of law, and the ultimate result.)

(3)   In the margins of the case decision in your case book, make notes opposite your underlining to denote each of the components mentioned above (i.e., facts, issue, rules of law, application of the rules of law to the facts, and result). As you are reading, also make a note of anything that strikes you as particularly important or confusing. And be sure to identify the particular legal claim or defense involved.

(4)   When you read a case decision, don't be surprised if sometimes you disagree with the principles of law set out by the court,

the court's application of the law to the facts, or the result in the case. Indeed, you should be thinking critically about the court's decision as you are reading. Remember that oftentimes the case decisions you will be reading are only "opinions" by a particular panel of a particular court, and it is not unusual for another (or higher) court to disagree and reach a different result. Thus, never read a case decision as having the same quality of correctness that we ascribe to, for example, the laws of mathematics or physics that are inviolate and always true. Remember that reasonable minds often differ as to the proper legal principles and application of those principles to the particular facts in reaching a result.

(5)   If you do find yourself disagreeing with a decision, you must identify precisely *why* you disagree. This is important because the reasons for your disagreement will reflect your understanding of the arguments that might be made for a different outcome of the case, which is another essential skill of being a lawyer.

(6)   When reading case decisions, ask yourself whether the legal rules, application of the legal rules to the facts, and result in the case make intuitive sense in light of (a) fundamental notions of fairness and reasonableness, (b) continuity of the law over time as a workable and practical set of rules in like circumstances (i.e., precedent), and (c) an appropriate balance of public policies or goals of the law in our society. (See Chapter 9 at § 9.01 about public policies in the law).

(7)   Finally, to emphasize (6) above, don't throw your common sense out the window when you are reading case decisions. This is important because many law students make the mistake of jettisoning their basic common sense and life experience when studying the law. Never forget that the law applies to real life situations. Indeed, the law is best *understood* when considered in its actual and practical application to the real world. (See Chapter

9 at §9.02 of this book for more about using common sense in law school.)

5.02 Examples of Reading Case Decisions

Below are excerpts from two case decisions, *Garratt v. Dailey* and *Masters v. Becker*. The excerpts have been underlined and annotated (with notes in the margins) as examples of how you should be actively reading your case decisions. You will notice that we have identified (as shown in bold underscoring): (1) the key *facts*, including procedural history of the case; (2) the *issue*; (3) the rules of *law*; (4) the *application of the law to the facts*; and (5) the ultimate decision or *result* in the case.

[1] *Garratt v. Dailey*

46 Wash.2d 197
Supreme Court of Washington, Department 2.

Ruth **GARRATT**, Appellant,

v.

Brian **DAILEY**, a Minor, by George S. Dailey, his Guardian ad Litem, Respondent.

No. 32841. | Feb. 14, 1955. | Rehearing Denied May 3, 1955.   *Claim*

Hill, Justice.

The **liability of an infant for** an alleged **battery** is presented to this court for the first time. **Brian** Dailey (**age five years, nine months**) was visiting with Naomi Garratt, an adult and a sister of the plaintiff, Ruth Garratt, likewise an adult, in the back yard of the plaintiff's home, on July 16, 1951. It is plaintiff's contention that she came out into the back yard to talk with Naomi and that, as she started to sit down in a wood and canvas lawn chair, Brian deliberately pulled it out from under her. The only one of the three persons present so testifying was Naomi Garratt. (Ruth Garratt, the plaintiff, did not testify as to how or why she fell.) The **trial court**, unwilling to accept this testimony, adopted instead Brian Dailey's version of what happened, and **made the following findings**:

Trial Court Facts

"III. * * * that while Naomi Garratt and Brian Dailey were in the back yard the plaintiff, Ruth Garratt, came out of her house into the back yard. Sometime subsequent thereto defendant, **Brian** Dailey**, picked up** a lightly built wood and canvas **lawn chair** which was then and there located in the back yard of the above described premises, **moved it** sideways a few feet **and seated himself** therein, at which time he **discovered the plaintiff, Ruth Garratt, about to sit down at the place where the lawn chair had formerly been, at which time he hurriedly got up from the chair and attempted to move it toward Ruth Garratt to aid her in sitting down in the chair**; that due to the defendant's small size and lack of dexterity **he was unable to get the lawn chair under the plaintiff in time to prevent her from falling to the ground**. That **plaintiff fell to the ground and sustained a fracture of her hip**, and other injuries and damages as hereinafter set forth.

"IV. That the preponderance of the evidence in this case establishes that when the defendant, **Brian** Dailey, moved the chair in question he *did not have any willful or unlawful purpose* in doing so; that *he did not have any intent to injure the plaintiff, or any intent to bring about any unauthorized or offensive contact with her person* or any objects appurtenant thereto; that the circumstances which immediately preceded the fall of the plaintiff established that the defendant, *Brian Dailey, did not have purpose, intent or design to perform a prank or to effect an assault and battery upon the per-*

son of the plaintiff.'

It is conceded that Ruth Garratt's fall resulted in a fractured hip and other painful and serious injuries. To obviate the necessity of a retrial in the event this court determines that she was entitled to a judgment against Brian Dailey, the amount of her damage was found to be $11,000. **Plaintiff appeals from a judgment dismissing the actionand asks for the entry of a judgment in that amount or a new trial**. *Issue*

The authorities generally, but with certain notable exceptions, see Bohlen, "Liability in Tort of Infants and Insane Persons," 23 Mich.L.Rev. 9, state that when a minor has committed a tort with force he is liable to be proceeded against as any other person would be. * * *

In our analysis of the applicable law, we start with the basic premise that Brian, whether five or fifty-five, must have committed some wrongful act before he could be liable for appellant's injuries.

The trial court's finding that Brian was a visitor in the Garratt back yard is supported by the evidence and negatives appellant's assertion that Brian was a trespasser and had no right to touch, move, or sit in any chair in that yard, and that contention will not receive further consideration. *Law*

It is urged that Brian's action in moving the chair constituted a battery. A definition (not all-inclusive but sufficient for our purpose) of a **battery is the intentional infliction of a harmful bodily contact upon another**. The rule that determines liability for battery is given in 1 Restatement, Torts, 29, § 13, as: "An act which, directly or indirectly, is the legal cause of a harmful contact with another's person makes the actor **liable** to the other, **if**

> '(a) the act is done with the intention of bringing about a harmful or offensive contact or an apprehension thereof to the other or a third person, and**

**'(b) the contact is not consented to by the other or
the other's consent thereto is procured by fraud or
duress, and
'(c) the contact is not otherwise privileged."**

We have in this case no question of consent or privilege. We
therefore proceed to an immediate consideration of intent and
its place in the law of battery. In the comment on clause (a), the
Restatement says:

> *"Character of actor's intention.* In order that an act may
> be done with the intention of bringing about a harmful
> or offensive contact or an apprehension thereof to a par-
> ticular person, either the other or a third person, **the
> act must be done for the purpose of causing the con-
> tact or apprehension or with knowledge on the part
> of the actor that such contact or apprehension is sub-
> stantially certain to be produced."** See, also, Prosser
> on Torts 41, § 8.

We have here the conceded volitional act of Brian, *i.e.*, the
moving of a chair. Had the plaintiff proved to the satisfaction
of the trial court that Brian moved the chair while she was in
the act of sitting down, Brian's action would patently have been
for the purpose or with the intent of causing the plaintiff's bodily
contact with the ground, and she would be entitled to a judgment
against him for the resulting damages. * * *

The plaintiff based her case on that theory, and the trial
court held that she failed in her proof and accepted Brian's version of the facts rather than that given by the eyewitness who
testified for the plaintiff. After the trial court determined that
the plaintiff had not established her theory of a battery (*i.e.*,
that Brian had pulled the chair out from under the plaintiff
while she was in the act of sitting down), it then became concerned with whether a battery was established under the facts
as it found them to be.

In this connection, we quote another portion of the comment on the "Character of actor's intention," relating to clause (a) of the rule from the Restatement heretofore set forth:

> "It is not enough that the act itself is intentionally done and this, even though the actor realizes or should realize that it contains a very grave risk of bringing about the contact or apprehension. Such realization may make the actor's conduct negligent or even reckless but unless he realizes that to a substantial certainty, the contact or apprehension will result, the actor has not that intention which is necessary to make him liable under the rule stated in this section."

Application of Law to Facts

A battery would be established if, in addition to plaintiff's fall, it was proved that, when Brian moved the chair, he knew with substantial certainty that the plaintiff would attempt to sit down where the chair had been. If Brian had any of the intents which the trial court found, in the italicized portions of the findings of fact quoted above, that he did not have, he would of course have had the knowledge to which we have referred. **The mere absence of any intent to injure the plaintiff or to play a prank on her or to embarrass her, or to commit an assault and battery on her would not absolve him from liability if in fact he had such knowledge**. * * * Without such knowledge, there would be nothing wrongful about Brian's act in moving the chair and, there being no wrongful act, there would be no liability.

While a finding that Brian had no such knowledge can be inferred from the findings made, we believe that before the plaintiff's action in such a case should be dismissed there should be no question but that the trial court had passed upon that issue; hence, **the case should be remanded for clarification of the findings to specifically cover the question of Brian's knowledge, because intent could be inferred therefrom. If the court finds that he had such knowledge the necessary intent will be**

established and the plaintiff will be entitled to recover, even though there was no purpose to injure or embarrass the plaintiff. *Vosburg v. Putney, supra.* If Brian did not have such knowledge, there was no wrongful act by him and the basic premise of liability on the theory of a battery was not established.

It will be noted that **the law of battery** as we have discussed it **is the law applicable to adults, and no significance has been attached to the fact that Brian was a child less than six years of age when the alleged battery occurred. The only circumstance where Brian's age is of any consequence is in determining what he knew, and there his experience, capacity, and understanding are of course material.**

From what has been said, it is clear that we find no merit in plaintiff's contention that we can direct the entry of a judgment for $11,000 in her favor on the record now before us.

Nor do we find any error in the record that warrants a new trial.

What we have said concerning intent in relation to batteries caused by the physical contact of a plaintiff with the ground or floor as the result of the removal of a chair by a defendant furnishes the basis for the answer to the contention of the plaintiff that the trial court changed its theory of the applicable law after the trial, and that she was prejudiced thereby.

It is clear to us that there was no change in theory so far as the plaintiff's case was concerned. The trial court consistently from beginning to end recognized that if the plaintiff proved what she alleged and her eyewitness testified, namely, that Brian pulled the chair out from under the plaintiff while she was in the act of sitting down and she fell to the ground in consequence thereof, a battery was established. Had she proved that state of facts, then the trial court's comments about inability to find any intent (from the connotation of motivation) to injure or embarrass the plaintiff, and the italicized portions of his findings as above set forth could have indicated a change of theory. But what must be recognized is that the trial court was trying in those comments and in the italicized findings to express the law applicable, not to the facts as the plaintiff contended they were, but to the facts as the trial court found them to be. **The remand** *Result* **for clarification gives the plaintiff an opportunity to secure a judgment even though the trial court did not accept her version of the facts, if from all the evidence, the trial court can find that Brian knew with substantial certainty that the plaintiff intended to sit down where the chair had been before he moved it, and still without reference to motivation. * * * Remanded for clarification.**

[2] *Masters v. Becker*

22 A.D.2d 118, 254 N.Y.S.2d 633

Susan **MASTERS**, an Infant, by Ralph Masters, Her Guardian ad Litem, et al., Appellants,

v.

Claudia **BECKER**, an Infant, by Nathaniel A. Kahn, Her Guardian ad Litem, Respondent.

Supreme Court, Appellate Division, Second Department, New York

November 23, 1964

SUMMARY

Appeal by plaintiffs from a judgment of the Supreme Court in favor of defendant Claudia Becker, entered January 7, 1964 in Nassau County upon a verdict rendered at a Trial Term (Thomas P. Farley, J.). * * *

Claim

OPINION OF THE COURT

CHRIST, J.

Issue   The single question is whether, with respect to a **cause of action for assault [common law battery]**, the definition of intent given by the trial court in its charge and in its ruling on an exception and a request to charge constituted reversible error. The **court stated that the plaintiffs were required to establish that the infant defendant** intended the act that resulted in injury, that she intended to commit an injury, and that she **intended the very injury sustained by the infant plaintiff.** The court also posed the question: "Can a nine-year old, by her action, intend the injury which resulted in this case?" To all this **plaintiffs' counsel took an exception** and requested the court to charge

Facts   that plaintiffs were required to establish only that "the act was done with intent to inflict an offensive bodily contact." The court refused such request to charge and adhered to its previous instructions.

When the injury occurred, the infant plaintiff **Susan Masters** was about **six years of age** and the infant defendant **Claudia Becker** was about **nine years of age**. They, together with Claudia's sister, **were playing on a motor truck** in an empty lot, and **Susan was standing on** a narrow ledge on the outside of the truck's **tailgate**. **Claudia told** or at least urged **Susan to get off**; and Susan refused and cried, saying she was frightened. Then **Claudia pried Susan's fingers off the tailgate and Susan fell to the ground, sustaining severe injuries.** Claudia's testimony indicated that the reason for her act was to force Susan to give Claudia and her sister their turns to get onto the ledge so that they could jump off.

Law   The correct rule as to intent is set forth in the American Law Institute's Restatement of the Law (Restatement, Torts, vol. 1, § 16, subd. [1]), namely: that intent is established "**If an act is done with the intention of inflicting upon another an offensive but not a harmful bodily contact or of putting another in apprehension of either a harmful or offensive bodily contact, and such act causes a bodily contact to the other * * * although** the act was not done with the intention of bringing about the resulting bodily harm." (See, also, *id.*, § 13, subd. [a]; 1 Harper and James, Law of Torts, § 3.3, pp. 215-220; Prosser, Law of Torts [2d ed.],§ 9, pp. 32-33.) * * *

A **plaintiff** in an action to recover damages for an assault founded on bodily contact **must prove only that there was bodily contact; that such contact was offensive; and that the defendant intended to make the contact**. The plaintiff is not required to prove that defendant intended physically to injure him. Certainly he is **not required to prove an intention to cause the specific injuries resulting from the contact.**

Application of Law to Facts

Hence, the trial court's rulings and instructions were not in harmony with the law. **On the facts a jury could** well find that Claudia intended only to force Susan off the truck, without any thought of injuring her. It could also **find that Claudia intended the bodily contact she was forcing upon Susan; and that, although this was not harmful in itself, it was offensive to Susan. Under a correct instruction, findings of the presence of such intent would be sufficient for holding Claudia responsible for the ensuing injury. In requiring plaintiffs to establish that Claudia in fact intended an injury and even the very injury that Susan sustained, the trial court was in error.** Such instruction imposed on plaintiffs an excessive burden and made it highly improbable that the jury would find in favor of plaintiffs. * * *

Result

As the error in the instant case was highly prejudicial, the judgment should be reversed on the law, and a new trial granted, with costs to plaintiffs to abide the event. * * * **Judgment reversed on the law and new trial granted** as between the plaintiffs and the infant defendant, with costs to the plaintiffs to abide the event.

Chapter 6

How to Write a Case Brief

Synopsis

> *When I have a particular case in hand, I have that motive and feel an interest in the case, feel an interest in ferreting out the questions to the bottom, love to dig up the question by the roots and hold it up to dry it before the fires of the mind.*
>
> —*Abraham Lincoln*

Chapter 5 provides you with instructions on how to read a case actively and closely. In addition to actively reading a case by underlining and annotating in your book, it is strongly recommended during your first year that you also prepare a written case brief for each case decision that you are assigned to read. A written case brief is a useful tool that will help you dissect case decisions and be better prepared to engage in class discussion. Some of your first-year professors may require you to prepare written case briefs and bring them to class. So, you are probably wondering: what is a case brief, and how do I create one?

A case brief is basically your summary of the case decision you were assigned to read. Your case brief should include: (a) a summary of *the key facts and procedural history* of the case; (b) a statement of *the issue and holding* in the case; (c) a statement of *the legal rules* pertinent to resolving the issue; (d) a summary of *how the court applied the legal rules to the key facts*; and (e) a statement of *the result* in the case. Without question, it takes time to write a good case brief. But, the exercise is well worth it—especially when you are new to the study of law. Writing a case brief forces you to summarize the case decision in your own words, which will help you to more fully understand what the court did and why.

You should know that some commercial enterprises provide pre-written case briefs for the case opinions contained in standard case book texts. You can also find pre-written case briefs on the Internet, or upper-level students may offer to provide you with their case briefs. These canned briefs are *not* recommended—we repeat *not* recommended—for two primary reasons. First, they are sometimes less than accurate. Second, and most importantly, they do not and cannot replace *your own* conscientious work in briefing cases. Briefing cases is a difficult skill that you must practice and master to learn the law, particularly in the first year. No effective shortcuts exist. Unlike undergraduate school, you can't succeed in law school by simply reading "Cliff Notes." You must do your own work because law school, done right, trains your brain.

This chapter explains each component of a written case brief.

6.01 The Facts and Procedural History

The "facts" portion of your case brief should contain only the *key* (more technically known as the "legally significant") facts from the case decision. So, what are the *key* facts? They are those facts that are *directly relevant to the precise* legal *issue* being decided by the court. Case decisions will often contain a litany of facts. Some of those facts are included in the decision to provide background and context, but they have no bearing on the ultimate outcome of the case. Such facts, therefore, are not *key* facts because the case would have been decided the same way with or without those particular facts.

When writing a case brief, your job is to serve as a filter—to sift through the court's recitation of the facts and include in your case brief only those facts that were *essential to or made a difference in* the identification of the appropriate rules of law, the application of the rules of law to the facts, or the ultimate result of the case. Remember, you are writing a case *in brief*. You are not simply transcribing everything in the case decision into a different format.

To identify the key facts, you must correctly identify the legal issues that are involved in the case decision. After all, if you don't know what issue the court was deciding, then you can't determine what facts were essential to the decision. For example, if the issue in the case was whether the defendant's conduct constituted the crime of burglary, the fact that the defendant was a college graduate would not be a key fact. Oftentimes (but not always), the dates or times that certain events took place will not be key facts. The court's recitation of the facts may contain certain facts that merely provide the setting of the case but, in the end, have little to do with the court's actual decision. Such background facts should not be included in your case brief.

You should, however, include the most important aspects of the "procedural history" of the case in your case brief. The procedural history is a description of the path the case took through the legal system. It will include such things as the pleadings, the motions filed, the claims and defenses raised, the rulings made by lower courts, and any verdicts rendered by a jury.

Here is what the facts and procedural history section of a case brief on the decision in *Garratt v. Dailey* (see the text of this case in Chapter 5 at § 5.02[1]), might look like:

Facts: The trial court found that Brian, age 5 years and nine months, picked up a lawn chair and moved it a few feet to sit in the chair. Brian then saw that Plaintiff Garratt, an adult, was about to sit in the place where the lawn chair had been. Brian got up from the chair and tried to move it toward Garratt to aid her in sitting in the chair. However, Brian was unable to place the chair under Garratt. As a result, Garratt fell to the ground and fractured her hip.

Procedural History: Garratt sued Brian for the intentional tort of battery. The case proceeded to a bench trial. Garratt did not testify at the trial, but her sister who witnessed the fall did. Brian also testified at the trial. The trial judge found Brian's testimony persuasive and found the facts to be as set forth above. The trial judge concluded that Brian was not liable for battery because he "did not have purpose, intent or design to perform a prank or to effect [a] ... battery upon [Garratt]." Garratt appealed, asking the court for either judgment in her favor or a new trial.

6.02 The Issue and Holding

After summarizing the facts and procedural history, you should identify the issue raised, as well as the "holding" for each issue. Identifying the issue and holding in a case decision is, at first, difficult for most first-year students; and you will have to come up with your own accurate statement of the issue and holding. Remember that the purpose of a case decision is to resolve a legal dispute between opposing parties. The "issue" is the *exact legal question to be decided by the court*. The "holding" of a case is the court's precise *answer* to the issue based on the court's application of the law to the facts of the case.

The issue in a case is usually, but not always, framed in terms of both the key rules of law and the key facts. If the issue is stated too broadly, it is essentially meaningless. On the other extreme, if the issue is stated by trying to incorporate all of the facts and propositions of law in the case into a single question, the statement of the issue may be too complex and convoluted to understand.

Issues take different forms depending upon the subject matter of the particular case. Often, the court decision itself will provide a short-hand statement of the issue or otherwise indicate the issue by stating the opposing contentions of the parties. In the case decisions you read in first-year courses, examples of typical types of issues include:

- the proper interpretation of a particular statutory provision, constitutional provision, rule of civil procedure, or legal instrument (such as a contract or deed) and how that interpretation should apply to the facts of the case;

- the sufficiency of the allegations in a lawsuit or of defenses or counterclaims asserted in an answer to a lawsuit to state a viable claim or defense;

- the sufficiency of the evidence in a civil or criminal case to establish the claim or charge asserted or any defenses to the claim or charge; or

- the meaning of one or more elements of a civil claim (e.g., the elements of a civil battery claim), elements of a particular crime, or elements of a particular defense to a civil claim or criminal charge, and how the court's interpretation of those elements applies to the particular facts of the case.

As mentioned previously, the precise *answer* to the issue is called the "holding." You should be careful not to confuse "holding" with "result." The "result" in a case decision is the action that the appellate court has ordered. It is often announced in the last sentence or two of the case decision. Typically, the court will express the result in terms such as "affirm," "reverse," "remand," "vacate," or "modify." A "holding," on the other hand, is a statement of the court's ruling on *how the applicable rules of law should be applied to the facts of the case.*

Consider now the issue and holding in the *Garratt* case. If the issue were stated "whether Brian is liable for battery," this statement is largely meaningless. To make the issue instructive, you must frame the issue in light of the key rules or principles of law stated by the court about the intent necessary to establish a battery and how the court applied those rules to the particular facts. Then the holding, which is the answer to the issue, will provide a succinct statement of the court's application of the law to the particular facts. For example, a case brief on this decision might set out the following issue and holding:

Issue: Whether an infant is liable for battery with the intention of causing harmful contact to another when, considering the infant's age, experience, capacity and understanding, he knew with substantial certainty when he moved a chair that plaintiff would attempt to sit down where the chair had been, and plaintiff was injured when she fell to the ground while trying to sit in the chair.

Holding: An infant is liable for battery with the intention of causing harmful contact to another when, considering the infant's age, experience, capacity and understanding, he knew with substantial certainty when he moved a chair that plaintiff would attempt to sit down where the chair had been, and plaintiff was injured when she fell to the ground while trying to sit in the chair.

6.03 The Rules of Law

In your case brief, the rules of law that the court has applied to the facts should be phrased, as closely as possible, in terms of the *actual language* used in the case decision. Here too, as in the facts, state the *key* rules of law—*those legal principles that are directly relevant to the court's decision.* For example, in the *Garratt* decision, a case brief might set out the following rules of law:

Rules of Law: A battery is the intentional infliction of harmful bodily contact upon another or a third person. An act will satisfy this intention if the act is done (a) for the purpose of causing the harmful contact, or (b) with knowledge by the actor that such contact is substantially certain to occur. Generally, an infant is liable for battery in the same circumstances that an adult would be liable. However, the infant's age, experience, capacity and understanding are relevant on the question of whether the infant knew with substantial certainty that his conduct would cause harmful bodily contact upon another.

6.04 The Application of the Law to the Facts

Your case brief should summarize how the court applied the key rules of law to the key facts. This is the court's reasoning— i.e., *why* the court reached its result. A case brief on *Garratt* might provide the following application of the law to the facts:

Application of the Law to the Facts: The trial court concluded that Brian was not liable for battery for the sole reason that he "did not have purpose, intent or design to ... effect a ... battery upon [Garratt]." However, the trial court failed to consider whether Brian was liable for battery on the alternative theory that he knew with substantial certainty that Garratt intended to sit down where the chair had been before Brian moved the chair. Thus, the trial court was obligated to consider whether Brian was liable for battery under this alternative theory.

6.05 The Result in the Case

As mentioned previously, the result in the case is the appellate court's ultimate decision to affirm, reverse, remand, vacate or modify the lower court decision, or other instruction to the lower court in light of the decision. A case brief on _Garratt_ might set out the following result:

Result: The appellate court remanded the case to the trial court to clarify whether, based on the facts previously found by the trial court, Brian knew with substantial certainty that Garratt intended to sit down where the chair had been before Brian moved it. In considering this question, the trial court should consider Brian's age, experience, capacity and understanding. If the trial court concludes that Brian had such knowledge, he would be liable for battery even though he had no purposeful intent to cause harmful bodily contact to Garratt.

6.06 Example of a Case Brief in _Masters v. Becker_

A full case brief on this case decision (see the text of the decision in Chapter 5 at § 5.02[2]) might read as follows:

FACTS & PROCEDURAL HISTORY

Plaintiff, a young girl, was playing with Defendant, another young girl, on a parked truck. When Plaintiff, who was standing on the tailgate, refused to get off the truck, Defendant pried Plaintiff's fingers off the tailgate and she fell, sustaining severe injuries. In Plaintiff's suit against Defendant for common law battery, the trial judge instructed the jury that Plaintiff was required to prove that Defendant intended the very injury sustained by Plaintiff. The jury returned a verdict for Defendant and Plaintiff appealed, contending error in the judge's jury instruction.

ISSUE & HOLDING

Issue: Whether a plaintiff in a battery claim is required to prove that the defendant intended to cause the specific injuries sustained by the plaintiff as a result of the defendant's harmful or offensive bodily contact upon the plaintiff.

Holding: A plaintiff in a battery claim is not required to prove that the defendant intended to cause the specific injuries sustained by the plaintiff as a result of the defendant's harmful or offensive bodily contact upon the plaintiff, but only that the defendant intended to cause the contact.

RULES OF LAW

For a battery based on bodily contact, a plaintiff must prove only that there was bodily contact, that the contact was harmful or offensive, and that the defendant intended to cause the contact. The plaintiff is not required to prove that the defendant intended to cause the specific injuries resulting from the contact.

APPLICATION OF THE LAW TO THE FACTS

The jury could have found that when Defendant pried Plaintiff's fingers off the tailgate, Defendant intended the bodily contact and that it was offensive, even if it was not harmful in itself. This finding would have been sufficient to hold Defendant responsible for Plaintiff's injuries had the trial judge not erroneously instructed the jury that Plaintiff was required to prove that Defendant in fact intended the very injuries that Plaintiff sustained.

RESULT

The court reversed the jury's verdict and granted the Defendant a new trial.

Chapter 7

How to Participate in Class

Synopsis

> *It is true of opinions as of other compositions that those who are steeped in them, whose ears are sensitive to literary nuances, whose antennae record subtle silences, can gather from their contents meaning beyond the words.*
> —Felix Frankfurter

A law school class will probably be unlike any classroom experience you have had before. The law school classroom is an active and rigorous environment. You don't simply show up and passively take notes as the professor talks for an hour. You will be expected—indeed called upon—to participate.

First year students often dread the rigors of class participation. This fear is fed by anecdotal accounts of law professors calling on individual students by name, mercilessly grilling them about the assigned reading, with the end result of reducing the students who have been called on to a puddle of embarrassment, humiliation, and bewilderment. Make no mistake: the law school classroom will intimidate you at first. It will also excite and inspire you. But, your professors are not trying to scare you; they are simply trying to train your brain for the practice of law. This chapter explains why law professors do what they do in class. It provides some pointers on effective participation and note-taking in class, and it will hopefully convince you that classes should be embraced instead of dreaded.

7.01 Class Objectives and the Socratic Method

Although law professors have different styles of teaching, they usually have three core objectives: (1) to make sure you understand the principles of law revealed by the assigned case decisions or other reading materials; (2) to make sure you understand how those principles of law apply in different factual situations; and (3) to expose you to the different arguments that a lawyer might legitimately make in support of a particular result in a case.

If you read and brief your assigned case decisions in the manner described in Chapters 5 and 6 of this book, you will be able to effectively participate in class. By that, we mean you will be able to respond to your professor's questions by reciting the key facts of the case decisions you have read and identifying the key principles of law. You will also be able to explain to your professor how the court applied the law to the facts to reach a particular result.

Your professors will also ask you "hypothetical questions." These questions will require you to apply the principles of law from the case decisions you read to entirely *different* sets of facts. Even though you have had no chance to read and specifically prepare an answer to the hypotheticals in advance, your professor will put you on the spot and expect you to formulate a coherent response.

If you hesitate or falter in responding to these hypotheticals, your professor may try to use a series of "leading" questions (i.e., questions that suggest a particular answer) to help you get to the right answer. Alternatively, your professor might reveal to you different arguments and ask you to analyze the merits of those contentions. In short, your professor will ask questions to probe your understanding of the nuances of the law as applied to different factual situations. Through these hypotheticals, your professor will also be evaluating how quickly you can think on your feet when blind-sided by an unexpected question. This type of teaching through the asking of questions is called the Socratic Method. Although some professors depart from the Socratic Method, it remains the predominant teaching method professors employ when teaching first-year courses.

The Socratic Method is named after the Greek philosopher, Socrates. Basically, it takes the form of questioning and discussion to stimulate critical thinking. The Socratic Method is *not* designed to embarrass or humiliate you. Instead, consistent with your professor's class objectives, it is intended to train you to: (1) appreciate nuances in the law and its application to different facts; (2) understand and anticipate different arguments that can be made about the law and the facts; (3) effectively express yourself orally; and (4) think on your feet when confronted with an unanticipated question from a judge or unanticipated argument by opposing counsel. In this way, the Socratic Method will not only help you learn the law, it will also help you develop practical lawyering skills. At first, the Socratic Method will seem strange to you. And, it may also seem as though your professor is "hiding the ball" in some strange game. With time, however, you will become familiar (and even somewhat comfortable) with the Socratic Method.

7.02 Pointers for Effective Class Participation

Below are six pointers for effectively participating in class through the Socratic Method:

(1)   As with most things, proper preparation prevents poor performance. To be an effective class participant, you must be thoroughly prepared for class. To be thoroughly prepared, you should follow the advice provided previously in Chapters 5 and 6, and bring your case book and case briefs to class. Also, if you

have trouble understanding a particular case or legal doctrine, consult a treatise or hornbook (such as the *Understanding* book on the subject) and bring the notes you took from the hornbook to class as well. Remember, there are no shortcuts. Class preparation takes time. But you will become more efficient as your law school career progresses.

(2)   If you are properly prepared, you will be able to thoughtfully respond when your professor poses a hypothetical situation that requires you to apply the legal rules set forth in the assigned case decisions to a new fact pattern. As you are preparing for class, you might think of what hypotheticals you would ask if you were the professor.

(3)   If your professor asks you to apply the law to a hypothetical situation, don't panic if the answer doesn't immediately come to you. You should not be afraid to provide a tentative response or to "think out loud" if necessary. If your professor follows up with a series of Socratic questions, do your absolute best to answer them. Don't give up. And, remember to listen very carefully to the precise question your professor has asked. Set aside your ego and don't worry about embarrassing yourself or saying something stupid. Remember that you are participating in an intellectual exercise that your professor has already thought through, but you have not. You are merely being asked to engage in a give-and-take about the hypothetical. The purpose of the give-and-take is to train you to understand and to articulate legal principles and their application to new fact patterns.

(4)   When your professor is questioning a fellow student, don't disengage or ignore the dialogue between the professor and your classmate. Instead, think about how you would answer the questions that are being posed to your classmate. Would you have answered the question the same way as your classmate? Why or why not? The key is to pay attention to what is going on during the exchange. Try to avoid becoming distracted, and resist the temptation to take verbatim notes of everything your professor

asks and everything your classmates say in response. Think of the classroom experience as a series of drills that are designed to train your mind, even when you are not the student being questioned in class.

(5) Ask questions and volunteer. Don't be afraid to raise your hand and ask a question if you are confused. If a classmate is struggling to answer a question and the professor has opened the question up to the whole class, by all means raise your hand if you think you know the answer. *Never* be afraid about giving a wrong answer.

(6) Don't hide in the back row. You want to be engaged and involved in the classroom experience. You don't want to be a "back-bencher" who tries to avoid engagement at all costs.

Class participation is something you should welcome, not something you should dread. If you daydream when you are not being called on by your professor, you will be missing out. Never view class as merely an opportunity to glean or speculate about what might be asked on a mid-term or final exam. The purpose of class is not to teach you how to take exams, but how to be a lawyer. Strive to benefit from the true intent of class—to train you in the special skills of thinking like a lawyer. This training will be enhanced if you are attentive in class, eager to participate, and unafraid to ask questions or volunteer answers. Let this protracted *process* of legal education work for you. Then, over the course of three years, your class time will be well spent, worthwhile, and entertaining too.

7.03 Taking Notes in Class

All too often, first-year law students try to make their class notes a verbatim transcript of everything said in class. You must resist this temptation—a temptation that is especially alluring if you are using your laptop or tablet to take notes because it is much quicker to type than it is to handwrite. Some of your professors will ban technological devices in the classroom, except for those students who have a special need for such devices. The professors who have adopted a technology ban have done so for a number of reasons — all of which are good faith attempts to enhance your learning. There is a significant body of research supporting the claim that students who take notes in class the "old-fashioned way" of paper and pencil retain information better than students who take notes using a laptop. And that is why in Chapter 4 at §4.05 we also urged you to consider writing your course outlines by hand. Although you may resist this as being somehow "old fashioned," remember the overwhelming research about the learning benefits of writing in longhand, which many lawyers do in actual practice.

Regardless of whether you handwrite or type your class notes, you should think of your notes as "short notations" rather than thorough notes. Notations are appropriate if, for example, they clarify something you did not understand about the law or how it applies to certain facts. Also, if your professor provides an explanation of a certain legal rule or provides some information that was not found in your reading, you should note it. Because most of your first-year professors will devote more class time to the Socratic Method than lecturing, you may find yourself taking fewer notes in some class sessions and more in others.

Chapter 8

How to Prepare a Detailed Course Outline of the Law

Synopsis

8.01 The Process of Preparing a Detailed Course Outline and the Content of the Outline

8.02 Summary of Steps for Preparing a Detailed Course Outline

> *Spectacular achievement is always preceded by unspectacular preparation.*
>
> — *Robert H. Schuller*

The preparation of a detailed outline of the law in each of your courses is essential to learning the law and studying for exams. Your outline must contain (1) precise and accurate statements of the rules of law, and (2) notes of examples about how those rules apply to different factual situations. We cannot overemphasize that your outlines *must* be prepared by *you alone*. This is imperative because the very *process* of *your* preparation of the outline is essential to your understanding of its content. That is, if you rely upon an outline written by another student or purchase a commercial outline, you will defeat the quintessential purpose of the outline—to synthesize what you have studied into a coherent, organized, and meaningful summary of the law that *you* will apply on your exams and as a lawyer. This chapter describes the process for preparing a detailed course outline and what it should contain.

8.01 The Process of Preparing a Detailed Course Outline and the Content of the Outline

The process for preparing a course outline consists of six steps:

(1) As explained in Chapter 5, when your professor has assigned cases from a chapter in your case book on a particular topic, you should first actively read those cases by carefully underlining and annotating them.

(2) As explained in Chapter 6, you should write case briefs on those cases.

(3) If you are confused by the cases or uncertain how a particular legal doctrine works, you should consult a hornbook or treatise such as the *Understanding* book that addresses that legal doctrine, and make notes of what you learned from the hornbook or treatise.

(4) You should attend class and take notes on what occurs during class. (See Chapter 7 at §7.03 about taking notes in class.)

(5) As soon as possible after you have covered the particular topic in class, you should take the information from your case briefs, hornbook notes, and class notes to prepare an outline of the rules of law on that topic. You should include examples showing how the rules of law apply to different factual circumstances.

(6) You should follow this process for each topic of law in the course and periodically organize your outlines on these topics under broader subject headings to eventually produce a comprehensive outline for the entire course.

For example, if your assignment is to read a chapter in your case book that deals with the tort of "battery" and contains the cases of *Garratt v. Dailey* and *Masters v. Becker* (see the text of these cases in Chapter 5 at § 5.02), you should first actively read and underline those cases, prepare case briefs on them, read and take notes on the battery section in a hornbook or treatise like *Understanding Torts*, and then take class notes. As soon as possible after the topic of "battery" has been covered in the course, use your case briefs, hornbook notes, and class notes to prepare an outline of the law on that topic. Your outline about battery might be as follows:

Battery

I. Battery is the intentional infliction of harmful or offensive contact with the victim's person or acting to cause such contact upon the victim. The tort compensates physical and psychological injury.

   A. "Intent" is satisfied if the defendant (a) subjectively desires such contact, or (b) knows that such contact is "substantially certain" to occur. The intent in (a) is commonly referred to as "specific intent," and the intent in (b) is commonly referred to as "general intent."

   B. The intent to cause the contact is the only requirement, and the defendant will be liable for the harm caused even if the particular harm was unforeseen or was not actually intended.

   C. "Offensive" contact need not involve physical touching (e.g., aggressive and demeaning grabbing of plate from plaintiff was a battery), and the victim need not be conscious of the contact (e.g., defendant who kissed plaintiff while she was asleep was liable).

   D. Neither "insanity" nor "infancy" are defenses (e.g., child is liable if he knows with substantial certainty that plaintiff will fall when child pulled chair from under plaintiff). An infant's age, experience, capacity, and

---

> understanding are relevant to whether the infant knew with substantial certainty that his conduct would cause harmful contact.

In this example, which is carefully written with both *precise and accurate* statements of the rules of law and examples of how those rules apply to different facts, the different subsections of the outline were drawn from the following:

- The first sentence of Section I comes from the *Garratt* case brief, and the second sentence comes from class notes.
- The first sentence of Subsection I.A. comes from the *Garratt* case brief, and the second sentence comes from class notes.
- Subsection I.B. comes from the *Masters* case brief.
- Subsection I.C. comes from examples given in the "Battery" section in the *Understanding Torts* hornbook.
- Subsection I.D. comes from the *Garratt* case brief.

In addition to the topic of battery, your *Torts* course will cover a number of other "intentional torts," such as assault, false imprisonment, intentional infliction of emotional distress, fraud, defamation, trespass, conversion, and invasion of privacy. After you have prepared your outline on each of these topics, you can group these topics under an overall subject heading called, "Intentional Torts."

Finally, never procrastinate in the preparation of your outlines. As soon as you cover a particular topic in the course, prepare your outline on that topic. And remember that sometimes you will find it necessary to re-write portions of your outline as your understanding of the law grows during the course. Set aside a regular time to work on your outlines, such as a particular day on weekends. Plan to have your outlines completed *no later than* by the last day of classes, if not sooner. Thereafter, during the "reading days" before exams, you will be able to devote all of your time to studying your outlines for your exams. (See Chapter 11 for how to study for exams.)

8.02 Summary of Steps for Preparing a Detailed Course Outline

Use the following steps in preparing your detailed course outline *during the course*:

(1) When your professor has assigned cases from a portion of a chapter in your case book on a particular topic, actively read the cases on that topic slowly and methodically by underlining and annotating: (a) the key facts and procedural history; (b) the issue; (c) the key principles of law; (d) the application of the legal principles to the facts; and (e) the bottom-line result or decision. (See Chapter 5.)

(2) Prepare case briefs on these cases. (See Chapter 6.)

(3) If you are confused by any of the cases or how a particular legal doctrine works, consult a hornbook or treatise (such as the *Understanding* series) that addresses the topic, and make notes on your case briefs or a separate set of notes about what you learned from the hornbook or treatise.

(4) Attend class and take notes on what occurs during class. (See Chapter 7 at §7.03 about taking notes in class.)

(5) As soon as possible after you have covered the particular topic in class, take the information from your case briefs, hornbook notes, and class notes and prepare an outline of the legal principles on that topic by writing *precise and accurate* statements of the rules law and notes of examples about how those rules apply to different factual situations.

(6) Follow the foregoing steps for each topic of law in the course and periodically organize your outlines on these topics under broader subject headings to produce a comprehensive outline for the entire course.

Chapter 9

How to Use Common Sense
When Thinking About the Law

Synopsis

> *The life of the law has not been logic; it has been experience.*
>
> —*Oliver Wendell Holmes*

As you begin your first year of legal studies, please remember not to leave your common sense at the law school door. This may seem like elementary advice, but experience teaches that it needs to be given. Why? Because for some students, the rigors of learning the law and applying it to new fact patterns has the effect of displacing all intuitive, experiential, and common-sense skills in the learning process. Don't let this happen to you.

As this chapter explains, if you consciously maintain and actively apply your common sense when studying the law, you will be able to (1) better understand and remember the law, (2) anticipate what the law likely is when there is no established law or you do not know the actual law on the particular matter, and (3) fashion arguments that are more sensible and more creative, which will allow you to be a more effective advocate for a client. Common sense is an essential prerequisite for good judgment. And good judgment is an indispensable lawyering skill.

9.01 Common Sense and Public Policies of the Law

Common sense is a short-hand phrase for "understanding how life really and usually works." A person with common sense understands how people typically relate to and interact with each other, how and why different values and beliefs affect individual and collective behavior, and how and why societal structures (social, economic, and political) influence collective behavior.

Consider, to name just a sampling, some basic beliefs and values in U.S. culture and society that are part of our common sense: fairness; even-handedness; the importance of notice, knowledge and access to information; equal opportunity and non-discrimination; liberty and freedom to think, believe, speak, worship, associate, and prosper as one might wish; freedom from fear, violence, and oppression; checks upon governmental power through a separation of powers among the branches of government; orderly procedures for resolving disputes; the presumption of innocence in the face of an accusation of criminality; the values of family, self-responsibility, autonomy, imagination, creativity, preserving the environment, and civility in public and private discourse. And there are many more.

Typically, courts and legislatures seek to advance these cultural beliefs and values. In the language of the law, these beliefs and values are typically referred to as "public policies." Because different public policies often conflict with one another, the law strives to weigh and balance competing public policies under the particular circumstances with sometimes inconsistent and frequently debatable results. But, these inconsistencies and debates about how the proper balance should be struck do not change the fundamental objective of the law, which is to *best* advance and balance our different societal values.

9.02 Reading the Law Through the Lens of Common Sense and Public Policies

When you read case decisions (see Chapters 5 and 6) or statutes or regulations, you will best understand the law in those sources if you read them through the lens of your common sense. In this regard, when reading the law, you might ask yourself:

(1) Does the general principle of law and its application to the facts of the case make sense in terms of fairness, reasonableness, and application to like circumstances in the future?

(2) What public policies are served by a particular principle of law, and what other public policies are perhaps being subordinated by that principle of law?

(3) How, and under what circumstances, would (1) and (2) apply to any *exceptions* to the general principle of law?

For example, when reading the cases of *Garratt v. Dailey* and *Masters v. Becker* (see Chapter 5), you might ask yourself the following questions: (1) Why is infancy not a defense to *civil* battery, but it may be a defense (or at least a mitigating factor) to *criminal* battery? Why would a person who commits a civil battery be responsible for all harms caused by the act, even if the person did not intend his act to cause the specific harms that resulted?

The answer becomes clearer when you think about the different public policies behind tort law and criminal law. Tort law, unlike criminal law, is not primarily designed to punish or condemn a person for his transgressions. Rather, the purpose of tort law is to compensate injured parties and to fairly allocate the burden of economic loss. Excusing an infant from liability or excusing a person from unforeseen harms caused by a battery would unfairly place the burden of loss upon injured victims, particularly when the infant or other person has assets to pay for the loss resulting from the tortious conduct.

Moreover, imposing liability upon infants and other persons for the full loss occasioned by their acts, incentivizes persons (as well as the parents or guardians of infants) to prevent harmful conduct and helps to ensure that victims are adequately compensated. Even so, as far as infants are concerned, the infirmity of youth is not entirely irrelevant to liability. As the *Garratt* case holds, an infant's age, experience, capacity, and understanding should be considered on the question of whether the infant knew with substantial certainty that his conduct would cause harmful bodily contact upon the victim. Thus, although infancy is not a complete defense to a battery claim, the impairment of youth may negate the intent necessary to establish liability.

Taking time to stop and ask yourself whether the outcome of the case makes sense from a legal standpoint, and whether the outcome of the case makes sense from a common sense standpoint, will help you to better understand and remember the law, anticipate what the law might be when it is undecided or you don't know it, and help you to develop sensible and creative arguments for what the law should be when you are advocating for a client. If you apply common sense, you might find yourself, from time to time, disagreeing with established law or a court's application of the law to the particular facts of a case. This disagreement is not unusual. You and your fellow students are the next generation of the nation's lawyers and judges; and through that generational change in legal practice, advocacy, and adjudication, the law will grow and change for the better.

Chapter 10

How to Research and Write a Memorandum of Law

Synopsis

> *The lawyer's greatest weapon is clarity, and its whetstone is succinctness.*
>
> —*E. Barrett Prettyman*

10.01 Overview of Legal Research and Writing

Legal research and writing are critically important lawyering skills. Regardless of your educational background, you are likely to struggle at first with legal writing. Why? Because legal writing involves both a language and a structure that is different from the other forms of writing you have learned over the years. Legal writing must be surgically precise and accurate. It also must be supported by legal authority, which is why legal research is a skill you must master. Legal writing determines actual, real-life consequences or decisions — whether by a trial judge or appellate court in deciding a case, or by a client in making an important decision. Given the importance of legal writing, there is zero allowance for vagueness, poetry, generality, or sloppiness in legal writing. The readers of legal writing (primarily judges) are also busy and impatient; therefore, you must get to the point quickly if you want to be effective.

Learning legal writing is also difficult because it involves two separate, but ultimately interrelated, components: (1) *what to say*—i.e., the content of the law and application of the law to the facts of the particular matter; and (2) *how to say it*—i.e., the language and analytical structure used for legal writing. The "what to say" component requires thorough legal research about the law. The "how to say it" component requires you to understand the typical structure and style of legal writing.

Keeping these two components *separate* is essential to legal writing. You cannot effectively write without *first* knowing exactly what to say, and then, and only then, putting it down on paper effectively. If you try to do both simultaneously—a common mistake—the writing process will be unnecessarily difficult and the final product will be poor. In order to know "what to say," you have to know the law. To know the law, you must research effectively. Part I below, therefore, provides you with a "Practical System for Legal Research." Once you know "what to say," you must say it in persuasive and organized fashion. Part II below will help you learn to do just that by providing you with "Practical Tips for Legal Writing."

Part I
A Practical System for Legal Research

10.02 Legal Research in General

Legal research is a skill. And like all skills, it is developed through study and practice. It is not sufficient for you merely to learn about the primary and secondary sources most commonly used in such research. Rather, mastery of the skill depends upon learning an organized system for using these sources and your repeated utilization of them in a meaningful way.

When you are asked to complete your first Memorandum of Law, you are likely to think: "What do I do now?" Your uncertainty will largely stem from confusion about what sources to consult first, which ones to consult next, what authorities to prefer over others, and how to preserve your research so that it is used effectively in the writing process.

A practical system for legal research can ease, if not obviate, that confusion. This practical system tells you how to get started, what research sources to consult and in what order, what authorities to choose, and a method for preserving your research so that it can be retrieved effectively when writing your legal memorandum.

Two caveats are in order, however. First, this chapter assumes that you have a basic understanding of the general content and utility of the research sources discussed. (This will be provided to you in your *Legal Research* class.) Second, the use of online legal research such as through Westlaw or Lexis is not discussed below. This is so because online legal research platforms vary significantly, and therefore you will need special training in these programs to use them effectively. (Your *Legal Research* course will provide you with some basic training in one or more of these online services.) However, you will be able to more easily understand and apply online legal research tools if you first know how to apply the legal research system provided below by using the books in the law library.

10.03 Getting Started and Identifying the Issues

As a threshold matter, you should remember that authors of legal documents are writing for a purpose. The most common purposes are to (1) persuade a trial or appellate court (e.g., through a memorandum of law or appellate brief); (2) evaluate the merits of a client's case (e.g., through an intra-office memorandum or client letter or email); (3) answer a discrete legal question (e.g., the statute of limitations in a civil battery case); or (4) write a scholarly article (e.g., for a law review or other legal journal or magazine). Sometimes these purposes overlap. It is critical that you understand the purpose for which you are writing because it will dictate the scope of your research and the ultimate content of your written product. Regardless of your purpose, your research should encompass authorities on both sides of your issues.

Usually, the first step in any legal research problem is to identify the relevant issues. Here, it is imperative to have a complete understanding of the key facts, and it is necessary to repeatedly remind yourself of those facts so that you do not go unnecessarily adrift in your identification of the issues and subsequent research.

Start by trying to identify potential issues intuitively. Ask yourself: "Can the judge really do that?"; "What is unfair about the factual scenario?"; "What areas of law might I look at to identify issues in the problem?" Similarly, at every step in your research and reasoning about the problem, continue to ask yourself whether the answers you are getting make sense. If not, further issue identification and research may be necessary.

On a more analytical level, issues may be identified by focusing on the following categories in relation to the facts at hand: (1) the persons or parties involved; (2) the item or subject matter of the controversy; (3) the timing and location of the situation; (4) the relief sought; (5) potential legal theories (claims and defenses); and (6) procedural matters. Issues may lurk within any one of these categories.

Next, separately list each issue you have identified. Your issues may initially take the form of general legal concepts. For example, on one page you may have written at the top, "Double Jeopardy" or, "Is the contract enforceable?" Then, on each separate page that lists a perceived issue, identify and list on that page West's Digest topics to research (e.g., "Constitutional Law," "Criminal Law," "Contracts"). If you are uncertain about the potential legal areas to research, consult a national encyclopedia (e.g., *American Jurisprudence 2d* or *Corpus Juris Secundum*), a state encyclopedia, or a state-law treatise on the subject.

As you conduct preliminary research, you will need to refine your issues. For example, the broad topic of "Is the contract enforceable?" may need to be broken down into sub-issues, such as "Was there a valid offer?", "Was there a valid acceptance?", "Was there valid consideration?" (see the elements of an express contract in § 4.04). These sub-issues should then be stated on separate pages with research-area headings such as "validity of offer," "validity of acceptance," "validity of consideration." Any one sub-issue may need to be broken down further. For example, "validity of consideration" might be broken down into research headings such as "adequacy," "forbearance," or "pre-existing liability."

Finally, you should not be surprised to find that identifying legal issues may be quite difficult in particular matters. There will be occasions when you are initially confident about your selection of issues, but later discover that your selection was misplaced. Thus, prepare to be flexible throughout your research. Above all, never lose sight of the particular facts of your legal matter. They are critical to the precision with which you identify your issues as a framework for subsequent research.

10.04 General Points for Preserving and Conducting Research

Whether you are conducting initial research for issue identification or detailed research after the issues have been identified, it is imperative that you preserve your research by writing down a *precise recitation of the law* gleaned from your research source. You should also write down a complete "Blue Book" form citation to the case or other authority establishing the point of law chosen. For example, if you are researching a problem dealing with the Eighth Amendment to the U.S. Constitution, your research recitation might read:

In *Weems v. United States*, 217 U.S. 349 (1910), the court established the principle of "proportionality" as a constitutional standard to determine whether a sentence is "cruel in its excess of imprisonment." *Id.* at 377. "Punishment for a crime should be graduated and proportioned to [the] offense." *Id.* at 367. While a court reviewing a particular sentence may grant substantial deference to the authority of a legislature to establish punishments for crimes, no penalty is *per se* constitutional and even a single day in prison may be unconstitutional under the particular circumstances. *Robinson v. California*, 370 U.S. 660, 667 (1962).

The advantages of preserving your research with the precision illustrated above are that (1) you will not have to re-read a case or authority that you previously researched, and (2) you will be able to directly draw upon and edit your recitation when writing your memorandum.

When conducting your research, focus on one discrete legal research area or issue at a time, not skipping from one to another. If, as you are researching one area of the law, you come across authorities or legal principles relevant to other aspects of your problem, make a note of those sources and read them when you undertake research on the issue to which they relate.

Photocopy or download a case or authority only if it is on "all fours" with the issue at hand, or if it has a lengthy quotation you want to preserve in its entirety. As discussed above, your written research recitations should otherwise serve as the raw material from which to write your memorandum, in lieu of an unmanageable stack of photocopied or downloaded authorities.

If you come across a case that appears to answer clearly the issue you are researching, immediately ensure that it has not been reversed or modified by a subsequent decision. (Check this for all other cases after you have completed all of your research and before you begin to write.) If your research reveals that the dispositive case is still good law, you may be able to stop researching that topic. However, you may still wish to do enough additional research to assure yourself that there is no other applicable authority and that there are no subsequent decisions that modify or limit the dispositive law relevant to your issue.

Finally, if you are consulting a source and finding it is not shedding any light on your issue, go to another source. If your research is thorough and methodical, critical authorities not found in one source will invariably turn up in another.

10.05 Researching State Law

When researching a state law problem, follow the steps below in the order given:

[1] Statutory Law

1.   First consult the index of the relevant state statutes and search it for all potential statutory provisions pertinent to your problem. List citations to these provisions in your research notes under the relevant issue.

2.   Read each statutory provision listed by going first to the supplement or pocket part, and then to the main volume. This step is critical because it helps you to be sure that the statute you are reading is current. Remember to read the whole statute, including definitional sections, any statement on legislative purpose, any editor's notes, and the effective date of the statute. If the statute is relevant, write down the pertinent language verbatim, along with the statute's exact citation. Only photocopy or download a relevant statute if it is long.

3.   Read the case annotations under each relevant statute (starting with the most recent in the supplement or pocket part), and write down the cases you want to read, using the citation to the National Reporter System (e.g., S.E.2d; P.2d; A.2d;, S.W.2d; etc.). Then read each recorded case (from the National Reporter System volumes), and write down a complete and accurate recitation of the law pertinent to your problem, along with a Blue Book form citation (including parallel cites) to the case from which the law is drawn.

4.   When reading these cases, also make a note of the most pertinent West's Topics and Key Numbers from the headnotes, and make a list of any decisions cited by those cases that you may want to read later. These notes will be incorporated in Steps 1 and 2 at Section [2] below.

[2] Case Law

1.   First consult the "Descriptive-Word Index" of the West Digest for your state, and search it for all potential Topics and Key Numbers pertinent to your problem. (Don't forget the pocket part.) Add these Topics and Key Numbers to the list you wrote down in Step 4 at Section [1] above.

2.   Read the paragraphs in the Digest under each Key Number (starting with the most recent in the pocket part and then the main volume), and write down the cases you want to read, using the citation to the National Reporter System. Add to this list any cases you wrote down in Step 4 at Section [1] above.

3.   Read each case (starting with the most recent cases listed from the pocket part) as published in the National Reporter System volumes, and write down a complete and accurate recitation of the law pertinent to your problem, along with a Blue Book form citation (including parallel cites) to the case from which

the law is drawn. Of course, if these cases cite other worthwhile decisions, read them too.

4.   If you find it necessary to research case law outside of your jurisdiction, follow Steps 2 and 3 above by using West's Decennial Digests starting with the most current volumes.

5.   Depending upon the nature of your research problem, it may be useful at the outset to consult the monographs published in American Law Reports (ALR). These articles may be directly on point with your overall problem. Always read the actual cases annotated in a particular monograph.

6.   If your research issue involves the interpretation of a word or phrase, use West's Words and Phrases.

[3] Other Sources

Apart from statutory and case law, you may find it useful to consult certain secondary sources. Along with issue identification, these sources may be extremely helpful in your research of the primary law. Thus, as appropriate, consider consulting (1) state or national encyclopedias, (2) state or national treatises, (3) Restatements of the Law, (4) law review or other specialized journal articles, (5) Attorney General Opinions (if they exist in your jurisdiction), (6) appellate briefs in published cases, and (7) law dictionaries.

10.06 Researching Federal Law

When researching a federal law issue, follow the steps below:

[1] Statutory and Administrative Law

1.   First consult the index of either West's United States Code Annotated (U.S.C.A.) or United States Code Service (U.S.C.S.),

and search it for all potential statutory provisions pertinent to your problem. List citations to these provisions in your research notes under the relevant issue.

2.   Read each statutory provision listed by going first to the supplement or pocket part, and then to the main volume. Examine the whole statute and any definitional sections. Read any editor's notes, noting the effective date of the statute, references to legislative history (e.g., United States Code Congressional and Administrative News), references to the Code of Federal Regulations (CFR), and references to treatises and law review articles. If the statute is relevant, write down the pertinent language verbatim, along with an exact citation. Only photocopy or download the statute if it is long.

3.   Read the case annotations under each relevant statute (starting with the most recent in the pocket part) and write down the cases you want to read. Then read each recorded case from the National Reporter System volumes (e.g., the Supreme Court Reporter for United States Supreme Court decisions) and write down a complete and accurate recitation of the law pertinent to your problem, along with a Blue Book form citation (including parallel cites) to the case from which the law is drawn.

4.   When reading these cases, also make a note of the most pertinent West's Topics and Key Numbers from the headnotes, and make a list of any decisions cited by those cases that you may want to read later.

5.   For statutory construction and legislative history, research the citations to United States Code Congressional and Administrative News that you wrote down in Step 2 above.

6.   For administrative regulations, research the citations to CFR that you wrote down in Step 2 above.

[2] Case Law

1.   First consult the "Descriptive-Word Index" volumes of the most recent West's Federal Practice Digest, and search it for all potential Topics and Key Numbers pertinent to your problem. (Don't forget the pocket part.) Add these Topics and Key Numbers to the list you wrote down in your prior research.

2.   Read the paragraphs in the most recent West Federal Practice Digest under each Key Number (starting with the pocket part and then the main volume), and write down the cases you want to read. Do the same with the earlier Federal Practice Digests. Add to this list any cases you wrote down in your prior research.

3.   Read each case (starting with the most recent), and write down a complete and accurate recitation of the law pertinent to your problem, along with a Blue Book form citation (including parallel cites) to the case from which the law is drawn. Of course, if these cases cite other worthwhile decisions, read them too.

4.   Depending upon the nature of your research problem, it may be useful (at the outset) to consult the monographs published in the federal edition of the American Law Reports (ALR Fed.). These articles may be directly on point with your overall problem. Always read the actual cases annotated in a particular monograph.

5.   If your research problem involves the interpretation of a word or phrase, use West's Words and Phrases.

[3] Other Sources

Apart from statutes and case law, you may find it useful to consult certain secondary sources. Along with issue identification, these sources may be extremely helpful in your research of the primary law. Thus, as appropriate, consider consulting

(1) national encyclopedias, (2) national treatises, (3) law review or other specialized journal articles, (4) appellate briefs in published cases, and (5) law dictionaries.

10.07 Weight of Authority

[1] In General

When conducting and preserving your research, it is necessary to develop a sense for which authorities (among the many that may be available) will be most persuasive in your jurisdiction. First, as a general rule, choose the best reasoned cases. This is important because a case that merely states a legal proposition is less persuasive than one that explains why the court adopted the particular proposition and reached a particular result. A glib holding, except on a well-settled rule of law, is of little guidance. Thus, on a controversial legal point, it does not matter so much if the case is older than newer so long as it is well reasoned.

Second, if available, try to choose cases with similar facts to your issue or, if you are distinguishing authority, cases with facts dissimilar to your issue or with reasoning that would not apply to your issue. Never choose a case with a similarity that has no meaningful parallel or a case with a distinction that has no meaningful difference.

Third, when you have a choice among a number of similar cases, choose a more recent case rather than an older one. Alternatively, if available, you might sometimes choose a case decided by a widely-respected judge in your jurisdiction such that the judge's own reputation might carry some weight that may spill over favorably onto your argument or contention.

[2] State Law Hierarchy & Federal Law Hierarchy

As a rough guide for prioritizing your choice of state-law authorities and federal-law authorities, the following constitute the most authoritative sources in descending order of persuasiveness:

Ranking of Authoritative Sources	
State Law Hierarchy	**Federal Law Hierarchy**
U.S. Constitution & U.S. Supreme Court decisions	U.S. Constitution & U.S. Supreme Court decisions
State Constitution in your jurisdiction	United States Code (U.S.C.), and Code of Federal Regulations (CFR)
State statutes and administrative regulations in your jurisdiction	U.S. Court of Appeals decisions in your jurisdiction (i.e., Circuit)
Decisions of the highest state court in your jurisdiction	U.S. Court of Appeals decisions from other jurisdictions
State intermediate appellate court decisions in your jurisdiction	U.S. District Court decisions in your jurisdiction
State administrative agency decisions in your jurisdiction	U.S. District Court decisions from other jurisdictions
State Attorney General Opinions	National treatises
Pattern Jury Instructions from your jurisdiction	Law review articles
State treatises in your jurisdiction	
State encyclopedia in your jurisdiction	

Ranking of Authoritative Sources, *continued*	
State Law Hierarchy	**Federal Law Hierarchy**
State appellate court decisions from other jurisdictions	
ALR Annotations	
State law review articles in your jurisdiction	
Analogous U.S. Court of Appeals decisions, and U.S. District Court decisions	
National encyclopedias, national treatises, and Restatements of the Law	
State law review articles from other jurisdictions	

10.08 What to Look for in Cases

Apart from weight of authority, there are certain types of cases that you should look for in preparing to write a memorandum of law. The most common types are as follows:

[1] Cases that State the Applicable Legal Principles

a. Cases that state the general rule of law.

b. Cases that explain or clarify the meaning of the general rule.

c. Cases that state the legal test for sufficiency of proof (e.g., preponderance of the evidence; or clear, cogent and convincing evidence).

d. Cases that state the standard for appellate review.

e. Cases with holdings rather than mere *dicta*.

f. Cases with pithy, quotable language.

[2] Cases that Clarify Statutes or Administrative Regulations

a. Cases that interpret the meaning of the statutory or regulatory language.

b. Cases stating the applicable rules of statutory construction when the statutory language is ambiguous.

c. Cases that speak to strict or liberal construction of statutes.

d. Cases discussing legislative history.

e. Cases construing similarly worded statutes.

[3] Cases that are Analogous or Distinguishable

a. Cases with similar key facts to your problem.

b. Cases with dissimilar key facts when distinguishing adverse authority.

c. Cases that are well reasoned.

[4] Authorities in Support of Changing the Law or Dealing with Unsettled Law

a. Cases with dissenting or concurring opinions.

b. Cases discussing analogous areas of the law.

c. Cases discussing policy considerations.

d. Law review articles.

e. Criticisms in treatises.

10.09 Finalizing Your Research Notes

After you complete your research, organize your research notes under each separate issue. For example, you may be able to collate all of your research on "Double Jeopardy" into one issue: "Did the trial court err in convicting and sentencing the defendant on careless and reckless driving when he had previously been convicted of driving under the influence on the same facts in a prior proceeding?"

Next, read through your research notes under each issue and cross out or discard those notes that are no longer pertinent or useful to the analysis of your issue. In this regard, keep in mind again the particular purpose of your research and writing. Conduct any further research if necessary.

Before beginning to write, make sure that all authorities you intend to rely upon have not been overruled or modified in material respects. (If you followed the technique of first researching the most recent authorities in the supplement or pocket part, it is unlikely your final research notes will contain authorities that were overruled or modified.) Nonetheless, final confirmation of the continuing viability of your authorities is essential to find out about any subsequent history (e.g., whether the case was affirmed, superseded, vacated, certiorari denied, etc.). As appropriate, add any subsequent appellate treatment to your citations.

Now you should be able to write your Memorandum of Law by drawing directly from your final research notes.

The key to effective legal research is to be methodical and thorough. The practical system discussed above is designed to facilitate these attributes. If you follow all of the steps suggested in the order given, it is very unlikely that you will miss any crucial authorities pertinent to your problem.

Of course, this comprehensive system lends itself best to novel and complicated legal research problems. Along with thoroughness, your goal is to zero in on the answer to your issue as quickly as possible. Thus, particularly when the subject of your research is narrow, it is entirely appropriate for you to employ shortcuts to the overall system. Experience is the essence of this efficiency. However, until that experience has been developed, the practical system detailed above will help advance your mastery of effective legal research.

Part II
Practical Tips for Legal Writing

10.10 Legal Writing in General

When students begin to write a Memorandum of Law, they often ask for one or more examples. Setting aside the particular format of the Memorandum, you will still want an example of *how* to write the *substance* of the Memorandum. If you want examples of this, they are abundant if you carefully *emulate* the structure and style of *recent* appellate court decisions. This makes sense because, after all, the authors of those opinions (as well as trial court judges and lawyers who rely on those opinions) are typically your ultimate audience. Thus, if you pay close attention to the substantive structure and style of recent appellate decisions, they will serve as excellent examples of how to write different components of a Memorandum of Law.

For example, if as part of your Memorandum you are asked to set out the FACTS of the problem, emulate the style used in recent appellate opinions when they set out the facts of a case. When you read those opinions, you will quickly see that the facts are usually set out as a chronological story based on the over-all evidence presented in the case. If in your Memorandum you are asked to set out the ISSUE in the problem, emulate how the courts sometimes phrase the issues in their opinions. (See also Chapter 6 at § 6.02 of this book for writing an issue.) Similarly, when setting out the law in your Memorandum and application of the law to the facts — i.e., the ANALYSIS — emulate closely the language that the courts use in stating the law and then applying the law to the facts.

Never be afraid of this emulation. If you think about it, most of what we learn is learned through emulation. This is how we learned to walk, to talk, to throw a baseball, and the like. So too, learning to write a Memorandum of Law is enhanced and informed by essentially copying the substance and style of the authors of case decisions. Moreover, because the authors of those case decisions are often the audience to which we write, our writing communicates best to that audience when written in the structure and style used by that audience.

10.11 Stating the Law and Applying the Law to the Facts

The most critical components of any Memorandum of Law are: (a) the facts of the situation; (b) the law; and (c) the application of the key law to the key facts to reach a result. Most students have particular difficulty writing components (b) and (c). With regard to these, keep the following in mind:

(1)   The law should be stated in one or more paragraphs *separate from* paragraphs that apply the law to the facts of the situation. Don't mix together your statements about the pertinent law with the facts of the situation at hand. Thus, you should write one or more paragraphs that state the applicable legal principles, citing to appropriate authority. Then, in one or more separate paragraphs, apply the key law to the key facts of your situation to state (or argue for) the result. As mentioned above, you will find that appellate decisions are written in this way.

(2)   When stating the law, liberally use the *actual words and phrases* used by the case decisions that you rely upon, and be sure to provide a citation to the authority that you rely upon in support

of your statement of the law. For example, assume you have written in your research notes that a particular case decision has defined the tort of intentional infliction of emotional distress as "extreme and outrageous behavior that is intended to cause and does cause severe emotional distress to another, where the defendant's conduct exceeds all bounds usually tolerated by a decent society and the plaintiff's severe emotional distress is a severe mental disorder or affliction diagnosed by a health care professional trained in such disorders or afflictions." Based on this language in the case decision, you might write in your Memorandum:

> Intentional infliction of emotional distress is extreme and outrageous conduct that exceeds all bounds usually tolerated by a decent society and that intentionally causes severe emotional distress in the form of a severe mental disorder or affliction diagnosed by a trained health care professional. [Citation to case decision.]

Note that 80% or more of the language used in your recitation of the law is drawn from the *exact* words and phrases used in the case decision you cited in support of the law. Note also that this makes your statement of the law fairly easy: approximately 80% or more of what you wrote was already written for you in the case decision, and your editing comprised approximately 20%. This is as it should be. Your statements of the law in your Memorandum should freely utilize the actual language of the case decisions you cite as authority for your statements of the law. This is essential for legal writing, because your reader will expect and demand that all of your statements about the law are supported by the actual law stated by court decisions, statutes, or other controlling authority.

(3)   In (2) above, the statement in your Memorandum of the elements of intentional infliction of emotional distress constituted

a recasting of the actual words and phrases of a published case decision without quoting the actual language of that case. Sometimes, however, you might find it useful in your Memorandum to quote all or a portion of the actual language used in a court decision. For example, in your Memorandum, you might alternatively write:

Intentional infliction of emotional distress has been defined as "extreme and outrageous behavior that is intended to cause and does cause severe emotional distress" where the conduct "exceeds all bounds usually tolerated by a decent society," and the severe emotional distress is "a severe mental disorder or affliction diagnosed by a health care professional trained in such disorders or afflictions." [Citation to case decision.]

(4)   Generally, it is often useful to include quotations of the actual language of case decisions in your recitation of the law when you want your reader to know the *exact language* used by the courts in setting out the law. For example, the phrase, "extreme and outrageous conduct" is vague, but this is what the courts repeatedly say. In addition, the courts routinely define "extreme and outrageous conduct" to mean conduct that "exceeds all bounds usually tolerated by a decent society," a phrase that is also largely vague. Quoting these exact phrases tells your reader that the definitional language you have used in your Memorandum comes *directly* from the *actual language* repeatedly used by the courts.

(5)   When the applicable law is stated in a statute, *always* quote the critical and pertinent language of the statute. This is necessary because the exact language of a statute is "the law."

(6)   When applying the law stated in your Memorandum to the facts of your situation, remember that this should be done in paragraphs *separate* from those in which you stated the law. Typically, you can begin those paragraphs with a phrase such

as: "In the instant case ... ;" or "In the case at hand ... ;" or "Here,
...." Again, you will see that case decisions routinely use these
phrases when beginning a new paragraph to apply the law to
the facts. Thus, after stating in your Memorandum the law about
intentional infliction of emotional distress, you might apply the
law to the facts as follows:

> In the instant case, John's rape of Mary constituted extreme
> and outrageous conduct because that rape clearly "exceeded
> all bounds usually tolerated by a decent society." [Citation to
> case decision.] In addition, as a result of John's intentional rape,
> Mary suffered severe emotional distress in the form of post-
> traumatic stress disorder, which was diagnosed and treated by
> her psychiatrist, Dr. Sessoms, for over a year. Thus, Mary has
> a viable claim against John for intentional infliction of emo-
> tional distress.

(7)   Sometimes, the facts of a particular case decision may be
similar to, or dissimilar from but relatively close to, the actual
facts of the situation that is the subject of your Memorandum.
In this circumstance, your recitation of the law might include a
discussion of the pertinent facts of that particular case decision
so that you can use it to either *analogize* or *distinguish* the case
from the facts of your situation. Note that this technique of arguing by analogy or distinction *only* applies if there exists a published case decision with somewhat similar facts to those
presented in your situation and where the facts of the case decision have either a *meaningful parallel* or a *meaningful difference*
to the facts of your situation. If such a case decision exists, you
must set out with *sufficient completeness* (a) the key facts presented
in the case decision to be analogized or distinguished, and (b)
how the court applied the law to those facts. This may take one
or more paragraphs. Then, beginning with a separate paragraph,

your Memorandum can apply the law to the facts of your situation. For example, if you are arguing by analogy or distinction, you might write in your Memorandum, as a separate paragraph:

John's rape in the instant case is analogous to the extreme and outrageous conduct found in Smith v. Jones, where the court held that a sexual assault, short of rape, constituted extreme and outrageous conduct that exceeded all bounds usually tolerated by a decent society. If groping a female's private parts was extreme and outrageous under Smith, then surely John's actual rape of Mary constituted extreme and outrageous conduct. To the extent John would contend that the decision in Alex v. Felix is controlling, where the court held that mere sexually-oriented gestures and comments did not constitute extreme and outrageous conduct sufficient to establish a claim for intentional infliction of emotional distress, the defendant's mere gesturing and verbal conduct in that decision bears no resemblance to the actual and forceful physical act committed by John here when he raped Mary.

10.12 Writing the Memorandum of Law

As mentioned previously, you cannot effectively begin to write your Memorandum of Law until you *first* know what to say, which means having conducted thorough research and having written down your research in the useable way described in Part I above. When you are ready to begin writing your Memorandum, strictly follow the steps below:

(1) Write the first sentence. Read it *out loud* (or read it by silently mouthing each word). If anything in the sentence does not make sense, is not absolutely clear and precise, or is otherwise wrong (e.g., spelling or grammar), edit, revise, or re-write the sentence.

(2) Write the second sentence. Read it out loud and edit, re-vise, or re-write it as stated in step (1) above. Then, read your first sentence *and* second sentence out loud, and edit, revise, or re-write as necessary.

(3) Follow the same procedure for your third and fourth sen-tences or any number of sentences constituting your first paragraph. When you have completed your first para-graph, read it out loud as in step (1) above and edit, revise, or re-write the paragraph as necessary.

(4) Follow the same procedure as in steps (1) through (3) when you write the sentences for your second paragraph and all succeeding paragraphs in your entire Memoran-dum.

The effectiveness of the foregoing method is that it dramat-ically improves the content of your writing by forcing you to edit, revise and re-write what you have written *multiple* times *as you write* your Memorandum. Also, the special technique of reading *out loud* what you have written helps you to write with greater clarity and accuracy by slowing you down and forcing you to determine whether what you have written is actually what you truly meant to say. This technique of *multiple* editing, re-vising and re-writing will produce a far superior product than would be the case if you merely wrote a first draft of your Mem-orandum and then read it over two or three times to edit, revise or re-write here and there. In sum, by following strictly the tech-nique given above, you will have, effectively, edited, revised or re-written your Memorandum tens of times rather than merely a few times.

10.13 Concentrating on Substance and Clarity

Many students, when writing their first Memorandum of Law, ask their writing professors not about how to articulate the *sub-*

stance of the Memorandum, but about details related to such matters as margins, spacing, type-face, headings, and other aesthetic attributes of a Memorandum. These "formatting" questions are legitimate and are easily answered by your professor. But formatting should be the least of your questions or concerns. A good Memorandum of Law (unlike what some students think makes a good undergraduate paper) does not depend upon how pretty the Memorandum looks. In legal writing, what counts is *what you actually write* and whether it is *clear, accurate, precise, supported by appropriate legal authority, and well-reasoned*—not whether you used indented margins for paragraphs or a particular font or method of pagination, all of which can be easily changed by a few simple strokes on your word-processing system.

Moreover, a good Memorandum of Law is one that is written in plain English. If you emulate the writing style of *recent* appellate decisions (as recommended previously), you will find that these case decisions are usually not filled with artificial, legalistic-sounding language, such as "thereto," "therewith," "hereinafter," "any and all," "including but not limited to," and the like. This type of legalistic jargon usually means nothing, even if it is too often still employed by some lawyers.

At the same time, however, you should always utilize the actual language of the law and its "terms of art." For example, courts do not define intentional infliction of emotional distress in terms of "despicable conduct," but by using the phrase "extreme and outrageous conduct." Similarly, courts do not refer (as journalists do) to "court papers," but refer to "pleadings" or "motions" filed in a case. Thus, write your Memorandum in plain English using the terminology of the law as phrased by the courts and shun any artificial effort to otherwise make your Memorandum sound "legalistic."

Chapter 11

How to Study for Exams and Write Essay Exam Answers

Synopsis

> *Do not on any account attempt to write on both sides of the paper at once.*
>
> —W.C. Sellar

For better or worse, you will have very few opportunities for formal assessment during your first year of law school. Unlike undergraduate school where you took multiple exams throughout the semester, in law school you will often have one single exam: the final exam (although sometimes you may be given a mid-term exam). Yes, that means your grade in a course will usually be based on one comprehensive end-of-semester exam. It is important, therefore, that you know what to expect when you walk into the exam room.

By and large, your exams will be comprised of essay questions. Some of your exams may also include a multiple-choice component. A law school essay exam will require you to apply the rules of law you have studied to an entirely new hypothetical fact situation. The days of writing an essay that is largely a regurgitation of information that you memorized are over. Indeed, you will be very disappointed with your law school grades if you simply regurgitate all of the law you know in your exam answer.

A law school essay question is generally a lengthy fact pattern describing a particular incident. Law school essay exam questions are similar in key respects to hypothetical questions your professor asks in class. In both situations, the professor is testing your ability to apply rules of law to a new fact pattern. To succeed on a law school exam, you will need to show your professor that you can do three things: (1) identify the legal issues that are presented by a fact pattern that you have never seen before; (2) recite the rules of law that govern the resolution of those legal issues; and (3) explain how the rules of law when applied to the facts dictate a certain result.

Most (perhaps all) of your first year exams will be "closed book," meaning that you can't bring your course outline or class notes into the exam room. However, sometimes a professor will allow you to consult your outline or notes during the exam. Even if your professor allows outlines or notes in the exam room, time constraints will usually prevent you from consulting your outline or notes during the exam in any meaningful way.

Your professors will typically give you advance notice regarding the format of the exam. Some professors may include exam format information in the course syllabus or will explain the format in class. If you commonly received a "study guide" from your undergraduate professors prior to exams, be aware that law professors do not provide "study guides." When a student asks a law professor "what do we need to know for the exam?" the professor usually replies "everything." And that makes preparing for law school exams a daunting task. To be adequately prepared, you *must* study *everything* you learned throughout the semester.

This chapter gives you guidance on how to study for exams. It also gives you a roadmap to follow when writing an essay exam answer. The chapter then provides two sample essay questions and answers.

11.01 Studying for Exams

As the legendary college basketball coach John Wooden once said, "Failing to prepare is preparing to fail." That adage is as true in basketball as it is in law school and also in life. You simply can't do well on law school exams unless you diligently prepare. You need to master the applicable law, and you need to know how that law applies to different factual situations. You can't fake your way through a law school essay exam. You must accurately and succinctly state the rules of law and then thoughtfully explain how those rules apply to the factual situation presented by the question to reach a conclusion about the outcome of the case.

To state the law in this way, you must memorize the rules of law that are set forth in your detailed course outlines. For example, you must be able to write: "Battery is the intentional infliction of harmful or offensive bodily contact. An act will satisfy this intention if (1)…, or (2) …" (See Chapter 8 at §8.01.) If you don't know the rules of law, you can't recognize legal issues and you can't conduct a legal analysis. Although everybody learns differently, there are several "tried and true" strategies for committing the rules of law to memory.

One common memorization technique is reading your course outline over and over and over again. Then, without looking at your outline, state to yourself (as if you were giving a lecture) the rules of law. If you typed your outline, actively interact with it by annotating and writing on it *in your handwriting*. For example, you might use your pen to underline certain definitions or phrases, put stars in the margins next to important points, circle key phrases, or make additional notes on the outline. Alternatively, you might handwrite a condensed version of your main outline. If you engage with your outline in this hands-on way, you will often find that you can literally "see," in your mind's eye, the notations you made on your outline when you are not looking at it. This is a very effective memory technique for learning your outlines.

Another common memorization technique involves creating flashcards using 3 × 5 note cards. With this technique, you essentially turn your outline into several stacks of flashcards that will help you to learn the rules of law. For example, you might create the following note card to help you learn the "elements" of a civil battery claim:

What are the elements of a civil battery claim?

front side of note card

1. Intentional infliction of
2. harmful or offensive
3. bodily contact
4. upon another

reverse side of note card

Once you have made your note cards, you can then test yourself by continuously going through the note cards until you have committed the rules to memory. You may find it useful to combine this note-card technique with the outline-review technique discussed above by using note cards primarily to memorize the "elements" of legal doctrines or definitions and by using your outline primarily to review how the rules of law apply to different factual situations. After memorizing the rules of law, some students test themselves by taking out separate pieces of paper and fully writing out what they have learned from memory. Choose the method (or a combination of both methods) that works best for you.

You need to understand that learning the rules of law is only the first step toward succeeding on a law school exam. Indeed, it is possible to "know" the rules of law backward and forward but still not perform well on a law school exam. That is so because your law school professors will not ask you to "list the elements of battery" or "explain the requirements for a valid contract." Your law school exams will require you to do much more. You will have to *apply* those rules of law to the factual situation presented in the question.

11.02 Steps to Follow When Writing an Essay Exam Answer

Below are ten steps you should follow when writing an essay exam answer:

(1) Read the instructions. As elementary as that sounds, it is something you must remember. The instructions are where you will find essential information such as time limits and page limits for writing your answer.

(2) Read the "prompt" (i.e., the specific question) at the end of the fact pattern. Then quickly read the fact pattern to get a general overview of its content. Law school essay exam prompts can take many different forms. Some are very general and will ask you to "identify and analyze every legal issue presented by

the fact pattern." Others are more specific and may ask you to assume a particular role in writing your answer. For example, a prompt may instruct you to "assume the role of the plaintiff's attorney and argue that the court has jurisdiction to hear the case." Given the variety of prompts, it is critically important for you to understand what your professor wants you to do in your answer. Remember, answer the *precise question* your professor has asked. Don't make the mistake of answering the question that you *wish* the professor had asked.

(3)   Read the fact pattern again. But, this time read it *slowly and carefully*, underlining key facts and making notes in the margins as you go. Read the fact pattern once again, if necessary. *But watch your time. You must reserve ample time to outline your answer and write a thorough answer.*

(4)   Take out a piece of scrap paper and quickly outline your exam answer. Your professor will be looking for a well-organized answer, and outlining before writing will help you provide such an answer. When we say law professors want your answer to be organized, we are referring to a specific organizational structure. That structure is commonly known by the acronym "IRAC." The acronym stands for Issue, Rules, Application, and Conclusion. More detail on each component of IRAC is provided below.

(5)   Once you have outlined your answer, it is time to start writing. As a general matter, you should consider beginning your answer with a short (one to three sentence) summary of your ultimate conclusion—i.e., your "bottom-line" answer to the precise question posed by the essay prompt. Be clear and be concise. You may find it easier to draft this *after* you have written the rest of your essay. That is desirable because, as you are drafting your written analysis, you may realize that your bottom-line answer should be modified.

(6)   Next you should identify the first legal issue presented by the fact pattern (i.e., the "I" in IRAC). By issue, we mean a legal problem that is raised by the fact pattern. Please be aware that

an individual essay question will likely present multiple legal issues. You will need to identify and separately analyze each issue. State each issue with specificity and in clear terms. Don't be creative here. Your goal is to let your professor know that *you* know what the legal issue is. You should consider beginning your statement of each issue with these words: "The first issue is whether _____."

(7)   After specifically stating the issue, your answer should explain the rules of law that govern the issue (i.e., the "R" in IRAC). This should usually be done in one or two paragraphs or more, if necessary, and you should use *the precise language of the law*. You will need to set forth the elements or components of the relevant rules. If there is disagreement among the courts regarding the controlling rules, you should mention that disagreement and point out which is the majority view and which is the minority view. A common question asked by first-year students is, "Do I need to memorize the case names?" The answer, generally speaking, is "no." Most professors don't expect students to cite specific cases in their answers (e.g., *Garratt v. Dailey* or *Masters v. Becker*). What you need to know and articulate in the "rules" portion of your answer are the legal principles set forth in the cases (or in the statutes or rules of procedure if they are involved). And this means that you must avoid a common first-year mistake known as the "law dump." A "law dump" occurs when a student simply writes out all of the rules he or she knows, regardless of whether the rules relate to the legal issues presented by the fact pattern. Remember, that you should only be reciting the legal rules that are *actually implicated* by the fact pattern.

(8)   After identifying the issue and stating the rules of law that govern the issue, you should apply the rules of law to the facts presented in the question (i.e., the "A" in IRAC). Identifying the issue and correctly stating the rules are important, but the application is the "meat" of your answer. In other words, this is usually where you can earn the most points. This is where you

explain to your professor *why* the issue should be resolved a certain way. Your task in this section of your answer is to analyze and explain how the rules apply to the facts. Don't simply rehash the facts. As you write the application of the law section of your exam answer, think back to your high school Algebra class. Do you remember being told to "show your work"? That same instruction applies here. When you write your exam answer, you should pretend that your professor is *not* an expert in the law. It is your job to walk your professor through the entire analysis, step-by-step.

(9)   Finally, provide a sentence or two that states the ultimate conclusion or result for that particular legal issue (i.e., the "C" in IRAC).

(10)   As recommended by Step (5) above, go back to the beginning of your answer to ensure that your bottom-line conclusion hasn't changed as you have worked your way through the analysis.

The steps above describe the IRAC analytical structure. If an exam question raises multiple issues (as it likely will), you generally should go through the IRAC process for *each* issue. So, you should start with the first issue, followed by the rules of law governing that issue, the application of those rules to the facts, and a conclusion on that issue. Then you would do the same thing for the second issue and so on until you have provided IRAC for every issue raised. Sometimes, if multiple issues are interrelated or the rules of law applicable to the issues are the same, you might state the issues together, then state the rules of law, and then apply those rules to the facts to reach a conclusion on each issue.

11.03 Sample Essay Questions and Answers

Below are two sample essay questions and sample answers to those questions. The questions are based on the case decisions in *Garratt v. Dailey* and *Masters v. Becker* that are discussed in

Chapters 5 and 6. Please note that the sample essay questions are more succinct than what you may experience in law school. This is so because the sample essay questions involve relatively short fact patterns and simple issues, but your law school exams may involve longer and more complicated fact patterns with sometimes more than two issues in one question.

[1] Sample Essay Question and Answer No. 1

QUESTION

Plaintiffs, Dalila Porter ("Porter") and Marsha Reams ("Reams"), each brought a common law battery claim against Defendant, Malcolm Dunn ("Dunn"). Because Plaintiffs' claims arose out of the same incident, both claims were consolidated for a single trial. The evidence at trial showed the following.

Dunn, 22 years old, is the only child of a widower and wealthy landowner who owns a massive horse farm. Due to a mental disability, Dunn has the intellectual and emotional intelligence of a five-year-old child. He received some education when he was younger, but he never attended high school. For most of his life, Dunn has been around horses and has worked on the farm, cleaning stables, feeding the horses, and doing other chores. Because of his mental disability, he has never been permitted to ride the horses.

Porter and Reams, both of whom are in their twenties, have known Dunn and his father, the owner of the horse farm, for many years. Both women frequently go to the horse farm on weekends to ride and exercise some of the horses. They describe Dunn as a "fun-loving" and "gentle" person. They often see him at the stables when they go to the farm and "joke around with him a lot."

One Saturday, Porter and Reams went to the farm to ride a colt named Rickets. After taking Rickets out of his stall and saddling him, Porter got up into the saddle while Reams held Rickets' bridle to restrain him. Dunn approached them, "laughing and carrying on." He held a bucket in his left hand and a broom in his right. While Porter was on Rickets and Reams was holding the bridle, Dunn hit Rickets on the horse's side with the broom. Rickets reeled up on his hind-legs, causing Porter to be thrown from the horse. The horse then trampled Reams before running off. Porter suffered a broken hip and shattered knee-cap. Reams suffered broken ribs, a broken jaw, and permanent scarring from a gash on her forehead. Dunn tearfully testified that he "never wanted to hurt no one" and that he was just "fooling around."

The trial judge, in his instructions to the jury, provided a basic definition of battery that Plaintiffs do not contend was error. The judge, however, further instructed the jury as follows:

> I instruct you also that in order to find the defendant liable for battery, you must find: (1) that the defendant intended to inflict harmful contact; (2) that such contact was in fact made by the defendant upon the very person of the plaintiff; and (3) that in making such contact, the defendant intended to cause the very harms that occurred. On the question of the defendant's intent as I have stated, you may consider the defendant's mental disability.

Plaintiffs timely objected to the instructions. The judge overruled that objection.

After deliberating for several hours, the jury found that Dunn was not liable for battery against either Porter or Reams. Porter and Reams have appealed, arguing that the trial judge incorrectly provided the jury with the instruction above. What should the appellate court rule and why?

ANSWER

The appellate court should reverse the judgment entered on the jury verdict and award Plaintiffs a new trial.

11 · HOW TO STUDY FOR EXAMS	129

The issues are whether the judge erred by instructing the jury (1) that liability for battery exists only if the defendant made contact upon the very person of the plaintiff, and (2) that Dunn's mental disability was a factor that could be considered when determining if he possessed the requisite intent to commit battery.

Battery is the intentional infliction of harmful or offensive bodily contact upon the victim. An act will satisfy this intention if the act is done (a) with the desire or purpose of causing such contact, or (b) with knowledge that such contact is substantially certain to occur. The defendant need only intend the contact or intentionally act in a way to cause the contact to occur, whether or not the defendant actually made the contact upon the victim. The defendant need not intend that the contact will result in a specific type of harm, and he will be responsible for all injuries resulting from the contact. In addition, because neither insanity nor infancy are defenses to a civil battery claim, mental retardation is also not a defense.

Here, the judge's instructions to the jury were at odds with the foregoing principles. Had the jury been properly instructed, it could reasonably have found that Dunn either (1) purposefully acted to bring about harmful contact to Porter and Reams when he hit Rickets with the broom to cause the horse to rear up and bolt away, or (2) had knowledge that this contact was substantially certain to occur. Although he had no experience riding horses, he had been around them most of his life and thus likely knew how they reacted when hit unawares by an object. The fact that Dunn made contact with the broom upon Rickets rather than upon Porter or Reams is irrelevant to liability because Dunn's act set in motion the harmful contact to them that occurred.

The evidence that Dunn was just "funning around," didn't intend to hurt anyone, and didn't intend the injuries that Porter and Reams sustained is likewise irrelevant. Liability for battery is not predicated upon these intentions.

In addition, Dunn's mental disability is no defense. Even if his experience, capacity, and understanding were relevant to whether he knew with substantial certainty that his use of the broom would cause harmful contact to Porter and Reams (which some courts consider when an infant is involved), a jury could reasonably conclude that Dunn likely had the experience and knowledge to know that Rickets would bolt when struck by the broom and cause harmful contact to Plaintiffs.

Thus, because of the errors in the trial judge's instructions, and because a jury could reasonably find Dunn liable to Porter and Reams upon proper instructions, the judgment should be reversed and the case remanded for a new trial.

[2] Sample Essay Question and Answer No. 2

QUESTION [Authors' Note: This hypothetical is based on the case of *Johnson v. Jones*, 344 P.3d 89 (Or. App. 2015).]

Plaintiff (a woman) and Defendant (a man) are medical doctors. Over time, they struck up a relationship. One night, when Defendant was over at Plaintiff's apartment, the couple had consensual sex. The event was initiated by Defendant. However, unknown to Plaintiff at the time, Defendant had genital herpes, an incurable virus.

Before Defendant's encounter with Plaintiff, Defendant had always disclosed his genital herpes to previous partners before having sexual relations. However, Defendant had never previously told Plaintiff about his sexually transmittable disease, and he knew that Plaintiff was unaware at the time that he had the disease.

A few days after the event, Defendant disclosed his condition to Plaintiff. Within a few weeks, Plaintiff tested positive for the disease. She thereafter experienced mental distress, depression, and anxiety; and she has suffered from on-going health problems as a result of contracting herpes from Defendant.

Plaintiff sued Defendant for common law battery based on the foregoing facts, which were heard by the trial judge at a bench trial. After hearing this evidence, the judge dismissed Plaintiff's claim because: "(1) Plaintiff failed to prove that Defendant had the intent to cause her physical harm by giving her herpes, and (2) Plaintiff consented to the sexual encounter, which is a complete defense to battery."

Was the trial judge correct (or not) in dismissing Plaintiff's claim, and why?

ANSWER

The trial judge was incorrect in dismissing Plaintiff's claim and should have found Defendant liable for battery.

The first issue is whether Plaintiff was required to prove that Defendant had the specific intent to give Plaintiff herpes in order to sustain a battery claim.

Battery is the intentional infliction of not only harmful bodily contact upon another but also of offensive bodily contact. Contact is offensive if it offends a reasonable sense of a person's dignity (e.g., the kissing of a person without that person's express or implied consent constitutes offensive contact). The gravamen of battery is the contact itself, whether harmful or offensive, and not whether physical or psychological harm was intended or results from the contact. Battery redresses injury not only to an individual's physical integrity but also to an individual's dignitary interests.

Here, Plaintiff's battery claim was based upon Defendant's intent to commit offensive contact and not his intent to cause the specific harm (herpes) resulting from the contact. As the claim was based on offensive contact, the claim was actionable even if Defendant's contact was not physically harmful, notwithstanding that such harm occurred. Thus, once Plaintiff showed offensive contact, a battery was established regardless of the particular physical or psychological injury suffered by Plaintiff.

The evidence supported a reasonable finding that Defendant's contact was offensive because, at the time of the sexual encounter, he concealed from Plaintiff that he had herpes and knew that Plaintiff, particularly as she was also a medical doctor, would not have participated in the event had she known of Defendant's condition. When Defendant had engaged in sexual relations with other partners, he had informed them in advance of his condition. Here, however, Defendant initiated the encounter with Plaintiff while concealing his disease.

Under these circumstances, even though Defendant may not have intended to give Plaintiff herpes, his contact was offensive and constituted a battery because his conduct offended Plaintiff's reasonable sense of dignity. Having committed the tort, Defendant was responsible for the resulting physical and psychological harm to Plaintiff; but the eventuality of that harm or Defendant's intent to cause it is not a prerequisite to Defendant's liability.

The second issue is whether Plaintiff's consent to the sexual encounter was a complete defense to her battery claim. Here, the trial judge erroneously concluded that Plaintiff's consent constituted a complete defense. This is so because consent procured by Defendant's nondisclosure of his herpes was no consent by Plaintiff at all. Therefore, the trial judge should have found that Defendant committed a battery by intentionally inflicting offensive contact upon Plaintiff that was not consented to by her.

Chapter 12

How to Make the Most of
Your First Year

For us, there is only the trying.
The rest is not our business.

—T.S. Eliot

Law school is difficult. There is no way to sugarcoat it. But, it can also be an extremely satisfying experience. It will be satisfying if you are prepared for class, participate in the classroom experience, update your course outlines regularly, and take advantage of the opportunity to learn from your talented professors and outstanding classmates. In contrast, if you are habitually unprepared for class, consistently shun class participation, continuously fail to keep up with your outlines, and consciously avoid interacting with your classmates and professors, then law school may become a lonely and unpleasant experience. And, more importantly, you may find yourself poorly prepared for the practice of law.

Be careful about feelings of stress and burn-out during law school. Sometimes, the demands of constant studying can be grinding, exhausting, and overwhelming. If that occurs, don't hesitate to take a break, to go for a jog, to get more sleep. If you try to study when you are exhausted, your efforts will be unproductive and largely futile. Practicing lawyers face periodic stress and burn-out too. But, with experience and maturity, they learn their limitations and how to cope with them by not pushing themselves beyond their reasonable capacities. Law school is good preparation for dealing with the stresses of real-life law practice.

You can reduce your stress by creating a study routine that works for you. Some students treat law school like a demanding job, working from 8 a.m. to 8 p.m. Others take an afternoon break, and then work several hours at night. Discipline is the key. The rhythm of your schedule will be your friend. Keep a planner if that will help to schedule your study time. Also, if necessary, feel free to avail yourself of the academic support programs your school offers. You should never be afraid to ask for help.

Cultivating a professional relationship with your professors will also enhance your law school experience. Professors welcome students who demonstrate attention and participation in class and who otherwise take the time to personally meet with them during established office hours to answer questions or seek guidance. Many professors are willing and able mentors, not only in the particular subject matters of their courses but in the professional development of their students as lawyers. However, there is one exception to this general disposition: professors are not particularly fond of students who seek them out with the sole motive of obtaining a particular grade in a course. Professors are interested in you as a unique student and as a future lawyer, not as a "grade grubber."

Your relationships with your fellow students are also important for an enjoyable and rewarding law school experience. Your colleagues are a resource for understanding the law when you need help, for uplifting you when you feel stressed, and for developing long-term professional relationships when you and your fellow students become members of the bar. You and your colleagues together constitute the new generation of the bar and someday will be its leaders.

The law is a powerful tool. When you are sitting in the law library at five minutes past midnight, two weeks after fall break, finals looming ever closer, looking down at your book, thinking you cannot absorb another word, and ruing the day you submitted your law-school application, remember that sitting there in that chair is a blessing—an opportunity that cannot be replicated. Remember that you are forging a foundation that cannot be feigned. Your skill cannot be achieved for free but must be earned through grit, sweat, and tears. Forget about the now. Ignore the coffee-stained book, your ink-stained hand, your weary mind. Instead, think about what is to come—the opportunity to become a member of a most noble profession, a profession where you will have the opportunity to use your unique skills and knowledge to positively impact the lives of others.

Index

basic skills, 37–38
case-law method, 38–41
legal research and writing, 38, 46–48
outlines/notes, handwriting *vs.* typing, 45–46
outlining, 42–45
reading, 36–37, 91–92
study groups/collaboration, 50–51
law school. *See also* class participation; exams, studying for;
law, study of
basic skills from, 37–38
doctrinal courses, 11, 38
first year, dealing with stress, 133–135
as gateway to legal careers, 7
grades, 48–49
legal research and writing in, 46–48
lawyers, work of, 8–9
legal analysis/legal reasoning, 37
legal research and writing, in law school, 46–48
legal research and writing, memorandum of law, 93–117
case law, 104
cases, 107–108
federal law, 102–105, 106–107 *fig.*
identify the issues, 96–98
legal research, generally, 95–96
memorandum writing, 115–116
overview, 94–95
preserve/conduct research, 98–100
research notes, finalizing, 109–110
secondary sources, 104–105
state/apply the law to facts, 111–115
legal research and writing, memorandum of law, *continued*
state law, 100–102, 106–107 *fig.*
substance/clarity, concentrate on, 116–117
tips, 110–111

Orders, *see* Memorandum Opinions
outlines, of law school courses, 42–46, 83–87. *See also* exams,
 studying for
 actively interact, 46
 class notes and, handwriting *vs.* typing, 45–46
 commercial outlines, 44, 83
 Contracts example, 43
 hornbooks, 44
 steps for, 87 *fig.*
 Understanding books, 44–45

P
petition, definition, 15
Petition for Writ of Certiorari, 19
Petition for Writ of *Habeas Corpus,* 32
plaintiff, definition, 14
pleadings, filing of, 22
preliminary hearings, 29–30
pretrial motions to dismiss, 22–23
Prettyman, E. Barrett, 94
probable cause, 16
Property, 11, 33

R
redress, definition, 14
relief, definition, 14
remand, 19
Reply, 22
requests for admissions, 23–24
requests for the production of documents, 23
result in case, 40, 55, 63, 65, 74
reverse, 19
rules, regulations and, 10
rules of law, 40, 55, 59, 64, 72–73, 125